The Science of Power

THE SCIENCE OF POWER

BY THE SAME AUTHOR

SOCIAL EVOLUTION, 1894.
    Translated German, 1895; Swedish, 1895; French, 1896;
    Russian, 1897; Italian, 1898; Chinese, 1899; Czech,
    1900; Danish, 1900; Arabic, 1913.

PRINCIPLES OF WESTERN CIVILISATION, 1902.
    Translated Spanish, 1903.

THE
SCIENCE OF POWER

BY

BENJAMIN KIDD

FIFTH EDITION

METHUEN & CO. LTD.
36 ESSEX STREET W.C.
LONDON

First Published . . January 25th 1918
Second Edition . . April 1918
Third Edition. . . May 1918
Fourth Edition . . June 1918
Fifth Edition . . . 1918

CONTENTS

PART I

THE FAILURE OF WESTERN KNOWLEDGE

PART II

THE BASIS OF INTEGRATING POWER

PART III

THE NEW PSYCHIC CENTRE OF POWER

THE SCIENCE OF POWER

PART I

THE FAILURE OF WESTERN KNOWLEDGE

CHAPTER I

THE GATHERING OF THE WORLD
REVOLUTION

AT some future time the nature of the drama which is at present unfolding itself in history must make a powerful appeal to the human imagination. Under our eyes, with the confused details of the transition spread before us from day to day in the events of the leading countries of the earth, we see the curtain rising upon an entirely new order of the world.

It is one of the curious features of our day that the nature of the change is as yet scarcely apprehended. The shadow of it rests upon all the events of the time. The meaning of it encircles the world. The instinct of it moves in the minds of distant peoples and of strange races. But there is yet scarcely any conception of its nature. We are undoubtedly living in the West in the opening stages of a revolution the like of which has never been experienced in history. We are witnessing the emergence of causes and the marshalling and leaguing of forces utterly unknown to textbooks. They will make history for a thousand years to come. But for the understanding of the great transition going on around us the very elements of thought do not at present exist.

It has been a feature of the time which has witnessed the greatest war in the history of the human race to talk as if the existing conditions of the West were the result of peculiar causes introduced by a single nation or affecting a single period of time. We must put aside such conceptions. The present conditions in the West are the result of causes which are universal, which have come slowly to a head in history, which extend far beyond military aspects, and into the meaning of which the development of the entire world will in the future be drawn.

It is a fact, the significance of which has been almost overlooked in the past, that Western civilization has been in a special and peculiar sense founded upon force. All the reasoned knowledge of the West is the science of force in one or other of its phases. Our civilization has been brought to the birth in time as the result of a process of force, which is unparalleled in the development of the race, and the conditions of which can almost certainly never be reproduced in history. For countless ages before history has view of him, the fighting male of the West has streamed across Europe in successive waves of advance and conquest, vanquishing, exterminating, overwhelming, overmastering, taking possession. The fittest, who have survived in these successive layers of conquest, have been the fittest in virtue of the right of force, and in virtue of a process of military selection probably the longest, the sternest, the most culminating which the race has ever undergone.

It is this fighting pagan of the world who has made the history of the West. The civilization which he has produced is the strangest flower in the fields of time. He has introduced into it at every point the spirit of the unmeasured ages of conquest out of which it has come. Into all the institutions which he has created he has carried the spirit of war, and the belief in force as the ultimate principle of the world.

But at the same time he has inherited a religion which is the utter negation of force, and which in every phase of his development has remained the outstanding challenge to his conception of the omnipotence of force. He has struggled with this extraordinary inheritance for centuries in history. Deep in the inmost recesses of his nature he has continually persuaded himself against belief in it. He has set his science and his philosophies to reason it away. He has gone forth on his business to the conquest of the world fortifying himself against it and with his spirit resolutely tuned to the doctrine of force. In his national wars he has made the right of conquest the ultimate right of the fittest. In the social struggle he has trained himself to see, in the steel claws of devouring tyrannies closing on the worsted, the natural law of efficiency.

It is only our lifelong familiarity with the outstanding features of our civilization, which has dimmed our vision to its altogether surprising features. As the spirit of the belief, which is the flat denial of the conception of the omnipotence of force, has gradually overmastered the worldbuilder of the West, the results baffle all adequate description. The pagan has captured the world by force. He holds it by force. But the system of ideas in which he is enmeshed flings into sight an unparalleled significance. While his philosophies have argued with it, while his sciences have branded it as foolishness, it has slowly enfranchised the world around him. It is bringing into the rivalries of life on terms of equality with him every class and substratum of his societies, every race of men on the planet.

The problems which are evolving themselves out

of the deep are illimitable. The blinding vision of which the West has caught sight has been that there is but one class, and but one colour, and but one soul in humanity. It is a vision under which the soul of the pagan world-builder flames in rebellion. But it has come to haunt the moods of industrial Demos as he hums his rag-time music in the midst of the mills of force which he has erected. The spirit of it moves in the dreams of strange peoples at the ends of the earth. And on the mind of Demos and of the distant peoples the effect is the same. It has brought a haunting sense of some meaning, infinite but unexplained, through which our civilization moves towards a fulfilment in which the past may pass for ever, and in which new standards of efficiency, that men have not dreamt of, may possibly arise in the world.

The male of Western civilization has become by force of circumstances the supreme fighting animal of creation. History and natural selection have made of him what he is. For at least four thousand years, and possibly for a period ten times as long, his forbears have represented the highest expression of force in the world. Every instinct of the fight, every quality of the rule of force exists in him through an ancestral inheritance measured by the meaning of hundreds of generations of successful fighting.

The consequences are felt to-day throughout every fibre of our civilization. As race after race of the peoples of the earth, as class after class, and layer after layer of their societies have been gradually brought into the struggle under the emancipating influence described, there has resulted a conflict of forces never before known. The problems thereof have become in every field of activity in the West the centres of movements molten with human passion. There has never been anything like the daily sequence of events which is spread before us in the record of civilization during the past half-century. It is a record of a war continuous and intense under every phase of human activity. In the programmes of parties, in the relations of nations, in business, in labour politics, in art, in literature, in the whole realm of economic activity, it is war in progress under every conceivable aspect.

But this cannot be the meaning of the West. Through it all there runs a sense of new eras, of new values, of emerging types, of widening horizons, of more spacious ideals of human brotherhood seen through the social emotion. But it is a world of revolution, of sinking temples, of falling idols, of rending veils, of darkening skies under which the gods of force huddle towards vast Armageddons muttering, " We know not fear," while the past moves from under them.

If we could only see the age which preceded the universal war of nations which began in 1914 as the historian of the future will see it, it would present a surprising spectacle, for we should see this war of the nations to be no more than an incident in a universal movement, involving every leading form of thought and activity in the West, gradually rising to a climax throughout the world.

There is a striking feature which we may perceive to be characteristic of the half-century which preceded the war which began in 1914. At the centre of every movement of opinion in the West the same fact is to be noticed. There is visible a gradual falling back upon first principles, a retreat all along the line to those conditions of elemental force under which the civilization of the West first came into being.

The Darwinian thesis, presented to the Western mind in the middle of the nineteenth century, had a remarkable effect on civilization. It presented to the masters of force in the West a conception of the world which they rendered exclusively in terms of force and struggle. It was not science which created the universal fame of the Darwinian conception. It was rather the half-informed pagan mind of our civilization. For centuries the Western pagan had struggled with the ideals of a religion of subordination and renunciation coming to him from the past. For centuries he had been bored almost beyond endurance with ideals of the world presented to him by the Churches of Christendom. He had stiffly bowed his armoured back to them, but mostly without inward comprehension. But here was a conception of life which stirred to its depths the inheritance in him from past epochs of time. This was the world which the master of force comprehended. The pagan heart of the West sang within itself again in atavistic joy. Its Schopenhauers, its Omar Khayyáms, its Haeckels, its Nietzsches, its Weinigers, its Wagners became the prophets and interpreters of a meaning in the world which it drank in with understanding.

There can be no more remarkable experience in store for the observer than that which comes to him if, in any of the leading countries of the West, he sets himself to compare at any of the centres of higher learning the questions being set a few years ago to students of the social and political sciences and those which were set in the same subjects but half a century before. The trained understanding reading between the lines beholds in progress a change far exceeding in significance any political revolution which has ever taken place in the world. The iron of conviction has passed from the mind of authority. The doctrine of force has taken its place. The ears of the present generation have been glued to the ground, strained to catch the distant meaning of vast, formless, approaching causes, speaking a language absolutely unknown to those who occupied the seats of knowledge in the past.

The full effect of the change long in progress in civilization has come into view almost suddenly. The significance of it was from the first perceived by the Churches, those historic centres for centuries of the idealisms of the West. It soon reached to every centre of opinion. For a prolonged period previously the Western nations, even in their darkest hours of struggle, had ever placed before themselves and regarded with unfaltering gaze an inward vision. They had conceived our civilization as gradually ripening, through the perfection of principles inherent in it, towards an age of universal peace and balanced harmony among all the nations of the earth.

The first startling effect in the West of the recrudescence of the pagan doctrine of the omnipotence of force was upon this ideal. For fifteen centuries, since the full adoption of Christianity by the continent of Europe, the scandal and paradox of the world, says the Honourable George Peel, was that European history was a tale of blood and slaughter.[1] But always hitherto this record had been shamed into irrelevancy by the permanence and supremacy of the vision in the background.

Within the short space of some fifty years all this has been changed. Those living have watched civilization becoming openly and of set purpose a universal place of arms. Within the half-century, by a process of development marking the intensity of the causes at work, they have seen standing armies, on a scale previously quite unknown, becoming a normal feature of the life of modern communities. The sun has followed its daily course from East to West over the nations of the world standing to arms and preparing for war. The full significance of the change, moreover, has lain in the fact that now it was preparation for war without any higher vision whatever of peace perduring in the background.

For the changes in the direction of thought have been far-reaching and rapid. The state of war became spoken of again among men not as a shame and a rebuke to civilization but as a state of nature. During the first period of the twentieth century

[1] *The Future of England*, p. 169.

in the reviews, books, newspapers, parliaments, congresses, and even in the schools of the principal countries, war has been the principal subject of interest. The discussion of war by experts and publicists—the methods by which war is to be carried on, the enemies against whom it may have to be directed, and the objects and policies for which it may have to be waged—has gone on continually.

As the result of tendencies which in a short space have enveloped the world, settled modes of thought regarding war, which in countries like Great Britain and the United States had been the slow growth of centuries of previous development, have become profoundly modified and altered. Men have come to listen silently, as they would not have listened half a century previously, when they have been told by leaders of opinion that the ultimate principles of civilization do not justify the prophecies since the beginning of our era as to an eventual age of peace and goodwill; that war is the natural condition of man, that it is not an evil but a necessity, and even a good, and that the modern resources of science are not tending to abolish war but only to render it more terrible and destructive by raising to the nth power the possibilities of savagery.

The alteration taking place in the nature of the pleas urged in favour of peace have become even

more striking and significant. Fifty years ago
the most prominent feature in the case for international peace was that it was made to rest on
the high ground of an immutable moral doctrine.
War was held to be a crime, a crime against the
principle of civilization, a direct challenge to the
fundamental conception of Christianity. It was
held, therefore, that the higher nations must evolve
beyond war, just as the higher individual has
been raised beyond crime, through the growth of
an internal moral standard producing a feeling of
absolute abhorrence.

But almost under the eyes of the current generation this view became replaced by another conception.   The high inflexible conviction urged
against war in the past, that the spirit of war was
a crime, that peace was a moral end to be sought
for its own sake and irrespective of any cost or
sacrifice whatever, ceased to be urged.   Peace came
to be advocated because it was said to be the condition which paid best in civilization; war was
argued to be economically unsound because it
was said to be a great illusion to believe that a
national policy founded on war could be a profitable
policy for any people in the long run.

In no phase of the time has the rapid lowering
of the standards of opinion in the West been more

directly in evidence than in this modification of
the principle upon which the demand for peace was
based. The degeneracy and futility of the argument which had come to rest the cause of peace on
no higher ground than this was deeply and instinctively felt by every mind which understood
the nature of the forces on which Western civilization rests. Even in the standards of those who
had begun to base the policy of nations upon the
omnipotence of force, the demand at least was
everywhere for the capacity for sacrifice.

The state of international relations in the West
for many years before the outbreak of the war
which opened in 1914 will be one to cause marvel
to students in history in times to come. We have
passed so rapidly through such moving events in our
time that the existing world has never seen in focus
the period through which we are living. It has
never fully realized that the great movements in
the West in recent times are but phases of a larger
development which in a generation or two has come
to envelop the whole of civilization.

The gradual lowering of the standards of opinion
and conduct has extended to all centres of Western
thought and action. But it was at the beginning
most clearly visible in international relations. One
of the most influential of British Liberal journals,

writing some years before the war, described in a vivid article the altogether extraordinary conditions which for a considerable period had come to prevail in European diplomacy. It seemed, the journal urged, as if civilization in Europe in the highest environment of culture had returned to conditions of primitive savagery. The crudity of the purposes, the danger of the aims, the thinly veiled barbarisms of the methods which were coming to prevail amongst diplomatists, were forcibly described.

Speaking of the conditions surrounding the diplomatists who were guiding modern affairs at the points of contact of the principal nations of the West, the journal with great seriousness continued: " We see them pulling wires, stealing marches on each other, laying long and crafty plans which almost invariably miscarry, and missing obvious events which throw all their designs into confusion. And on one side or the other there is a perpetual exploiting of the inherent loyalty and patriotism of their countries in quarrels which are mere combativeness for no purpose." In international relations, in short, the minds of the men of leading and culture who were guiding the affairs of the West seemed to the journal in question to have returned so near to a state of primitive barbarism that the journal gravely wondered why the immense majority in the nations did not assert themselves and sweep it all away.[1]

Whatever these symptoms might imply in their more immediate relations there could be even then no mistaking their import in the deeper aspects of history. The West was getting down to the first principles of force. The powers which had command of force were, with a sure instinct, preparing for a stage in which strength would be measured again in the West in those conditions of primitive force which the West understood. But the times were evidently pregnant with a wider meaning than this. It was a period more elemental still in which some new, vast, and fundamental conditions were assembling in the world, presently to emerge into full view in another era of civilization.

When we turn from these external symptoms to the social conditions existing within the frontiers of the nations before the outbreak of the war of 1914, the spectacle becomes more arresting. The world-wide reach of the revolution which has been in progress becomes more clearly visible.

For centuries it had been a commonplace of political thought in the West that the world that is, represents the world that always will be. The masters of force from the beginning took the Dar-

[1] *Westminster Gazette,* 31 October 1911.

winian conception as giving lasting support to the
view that the social struggle supplied the stern, inevitable condition out of which social efficiency emerged.
They took it as confirming that theory of the world,
which was already presented in economic science,
according to which the natural and unchangeable
condition of society was one of extreme polarity.
At one end there was the accumulation of property
and influence in the hands of the few representing
the leaders and the capables, and at the other
end there was the vast majority of the population
ruled down by the iron necessities of the competitive
struggle to the lowest wage at which they would
work efficiently and reproduce themselves.

In little more than the lifetime of a generation
we have seen the foundations of this world of knowledge transformed.   The emancipating influence
at work in civilization has gradually brought to
the multitudes the political enfranchisement inherent from the beginning in the conception of
human equality and human brotherhood.   In every
leading country the working millions constituting
the greater part of the population were to be seen
becoming consolidated and organized by the actual
mechanism of the process in which they were caught,
with the gift of political power in their hands,
with the dawning light of an intelligence in their

eyes never before seen in history, crowding at last at the head of every avenue of authority and stretching out waiting and impatient hands towards all the levers of power in the State.   And in the day-dreams of this multitude the sombre, insistent, infinitely widening instinct of the social emotion has already begun to close with the vast problems of the future.

Writers and historians will attempt in days to come to limn the bold outlines of the world drama in which we behold Demos in the West with the inheritance behind him of thousands of generations of successful fighting awaking in history in this situation.   It is a position with every element of human passion, every element of tragedy, every element of revolution in it, and all represented on a scale without precedent or comparison in the past.

Throughout the West it may be observed that for generations the idea of the world presented by textbooks of economic science has been based on a central conception.   However deftly the realisms of the human struggle have been glossed over, however faithfully the artists of its apologies may have softened the grim silhouettes of that struggle into a background of the public weal, of one thing there can be no doubt.   The fundamental idea of the economic science of the West has always been the conception of society as a state of war.

And in this state of war the central figure has been none other than that of Demos himself as the victim of it. The leaders of the proletariat as they gradually took in the details of the position have not been slow to interpret it to the masses in their own version. Every textbook of economics in the West, it was said, presented the same picture of the toil-stained millions. In the struggle of the world the overlords of the capitalist age of force took all they were able to hold as the wages of capacity. And the millions of the wage-earners were scaled down to the minimum condition of existence upon which the great beast of the proletariat would consent to reproduce its useful kind. That has been the rendering.

But the masses of the West have been themselves, and in their own right, and no less than the overlords of capital, the inheritors of the spirit of the ages of fight and conquest out of which the West has come. Gradually as they have drunk in with their new-born political consciousness the position thus explained to them, a new spirit passed over the West of the like of which and of the significance of which the world has had no previous experience. Firmly and consciously the hand of the working multitude has stiffened on the levers of supreme power which they have come to grasp under the forms of Democracy in the West.

The leading features of a position which moves towards greater events than any recorded in the past of the world may be rapidly summed up. There was no long parleying with the situation. The leaders of the proletariat went straight to the centre of it. History will record of them that without hesitation they simply accepted the world which the economists and the interpreters of Darwin had thus rendered to them in terms of force. But they accepted it with one reservation, the significance of which has begun to overshadow all the events of Western civilization. It became the avowed intention and determination of the leaders of the proletariat so to use the weapons which the political power of labour had placed in their hands that the result of the social war should be entirely changed. It should no longer be against their class ; it should be in favour of it. There can be no mistaking the wider bearing of such a resolution. Under its inspiration the movement of the proletariat in all the leading countries of the West has gradually taken on a meaning in keeping with the character of the general world movement in which all the institutions of civilization have become involved in our time. It has begun to present all the same symptoms of a development slowly concentrating on first principles, namely, on those actualities of force which are deeply inherent in it.

As we turn to watch the character of the international situation contemporaneously developing, we have to observe how the cause of the working classes of civilization gradually becomes involved as part of the universal movement in progress in the West.

Historians of the future will note that it took roughly the whole span of the nineteenth century for the masters of force in Europe, while remaining carefully hidden behind the screen of our current civilization, to evolve the principles of force scientifically applied in international war. The fundamental condition of the science of force as applied among nations was that which, first systematically developed by Prussia, has changed the face of the modern world, namely, universal conscription or the compulsory levying of the whole available male population of a nation for purposes of war.

The second and equally fundamental condition of force scientifically applied has been the gradual formulation, also behind the screen of a civilization founded on the ethics of the Christian religion, of the original code of pagan ethics which placed the interests of the State resting on force above all principles of universal Right and Justice. The great aim and object of scientific war as set forth in textbooks, now notorious, of the military nations of Western Europe, was to be successful. Every means to that end was, in the last resort, held to be justifiable. All questions of right, of feeling, of justice, of the sanctity of agreements or treaties, or even of humanity, became, in the last issue, nothing more than questions of expediency or the reverse in aiming at success.

Our time has witnessed the fighting leaders of races with unmeasured ages of conquest behind them turning in the middle of current civilization with the silent joy of the essential pagan to the stupendous task of organizing all the accumulated resources of the world to the making of war on these principles. The first outward result of a gradual return to the standards of savagery in European diplomacy has just been described. The next world-shaking chapter in the international position was about to open. But the conditions in which we have to witness the labour movement in the social war becoming involved in all countries in the same cycle of events have an extraordinary interest.

It has been said that the first principle upon which the supreme overlords of force had, with far-seeing vision, based all their plans for the organization of international war was universal military conscription. It has to be remarked that the first object at which the leaders of labour with the same supreme instinct of the fight upon them aimed in the West, indicated an insight equally clear. The first demand of labour was for nothing less than the compulsory organization of its own class throughout all the nations. Those who do not understand the magnitude of the position towards which the proletariat of the West has attempted to move in our times, and who do not therefore perceive the vitality to labour not only of organization but of compulsory organization, often miss the peculiar but fundamental feature of the struggle which has been opened. A study of the democratic State as it has been in history no longer supplies us with any clue to the future. It is the state of war between nations which henceforward furnishes the only parallel for enlightenment on the principles which control the existing class war in the West.

In many parts of the Western world the observer sees labour still under the old conditions of its struggle with capital, using the weapon of the local strike, throwing down its tools and engaging in feats of endurance to obtain by collective bargaining better terms than could be obtained by individuals.

But in reality this era of the struggle has been left behind in the main movement where the struggle with capital has now begun to converge upon essentials and fundamentals.

The principal leaders of the proletariat in the West have hitherto shown an extremely far-reaching grasp of the conditions and the limitations in our civilization of a struggle resting ultimately on force and conducted on a world-wide scale. By all the principles of effective war labour was bound to make a most determined effort to obtain exactly that same first object which the masters of military force in international war had attained by universal conscription. Its leaders proceeded, therefore, to secure throughout the world the first tremendous principle of solidarity for which labour stands. They formulated the programme known as the " closed shop."

This is, in effect, nothing more or less than the demand that no workman shall ultimately earn his livelihood without first being a member of a trade union. It is the history of the war to secure this fundamental object of labour which constitutes the real history of the labour movement during recent times. At one end of the scale we see the first phase of the struggle still represented in the United States, where the effort of labour to enforce this hitherto illegal demand for the closed shop has been accompanied for years by riots, outrages, and bloodshed, which have deeply disturbed the public mind of a continent. At the other end of the scale the struggle is represented in Great Britain by the example of the cotton trade, where in the most highly organized industry in the world the principle of the closed shop is to be seen emerging at last as a successfully established objective of labour. The world has, indeed, actually witnessed in recent times the operatives of this industry, having successfully insisted in the full daylight of legality that capital shall employ no workers who are not members of their union, proceeding completely to hold up the premier manufacturing industry of civilization for such a period as the exigencies of their warfare demanded.

The interval between these two stages in securing this, the cardinal position of the labour movement in the West, has represented a large part of the internal history of the leading nations of the world for a generation. The struggle has been in progress throughout Europe and America. It has furnished the principal events for a considerable period in the politics of countries like Australia and New Zealand. And it has everywhere presented the same features of a universal struggle in which a movement representing world-wide and fundamental interests in civilization is tending to fall back upon the prime and elemental conditions of force underlying it.

As the conditions of force governing the struggle have rapidly developed it has become visible how vital, how far-reaching, and how true to type has been the military instinct of labour. The principles of the democratic State from this stage forward begin to be pressed one by one into the background. One of the most effective and hardly won of the instruments of Democracy in recent times for the protection of right against force was the secret ballot in the election of political representatives. At an early stage in its own struggle we see the *open* ballot in the election of its representatives becoming a characteristic demand in the labour movement. In other leading features the transition of the movement towards principles of ulterior force of the kind which were being worked out elsewhere in military textbooks was rapid.

The press of the leading countries of the West for several years preceding the outbreak of the great world war of the nations in 1914 presents in this respect a most remarkable spectacle. Its leading organs are to be seen registering the opinion that a new era of civilization was arising under the prevailing conditions. Hitherto one of the most

pronounced of all aspects of legality in the West
had been the accepted sanctity of agreements.
But in the course of the labour struggle it began to
be a subject exciting profound feeling that in the
agreements made by organized labour on the one
side, and organized capital on the other, this principle
was often no longer observed.   The *Times*, surveying
in England the labour movement for a number of
years,[1] laid great stress on this remarkable feature,
maintaining that in a long series of crises legal
contracts deliberately entered into by labour had
been " continuously violated as if they had meant
nothing at all."

In these violations of agreements, moreover,
remarkable features were pointed out.   They were
all ultimately condoned.   The enormous voting
power of labour in the State rendered any other
action impossible.   A still more striking feature,
showing the retreat on the ultimate principles of
force which was taking place, was the nature of the
defence coming to be urged for these breaches
of contract by labour.   The proletariat, in a state
of war, it was said, had often no option but to
accept for the time being the terms of capital.
But, as it began to be characteristically put on behalf of labour, " a defeated nation may have to sue

[1] *Times*, 26 January 1912 and 27 March 1912.

for peace, and if the conquerors exact hard terms a defeated nation will, at the first favourable opportunity, repudiate such terms—and so with the men."[1]

Here it will be seen we are face to face with the standards of international war, where all conditions of legality have come to rest on force. We are, indeed, in the presence of that last argument already being advocated under many forms in the official military textbooks of the central States of Europe in which expediency had become the sole criterion of conduct directed to the end of success in war at any cost whatever.

There need be no desire to attribute to the responsible leaders or to the body of the rank and file of the labour movement in the West a conscious intent or consent to these lowering of standards. Enormous forces of quite a contrary direction were, indeed, behind the labour programme. What we are watching is rather the labour movement as a whole becoming enveloped in the irresistible tendencies of the universal movement in civilization which was now everywhere falling back rapidly on the actualities of force inherent in it. As syndical-

[1] Cf. "When a class issue of any importance is raised, Might makes Right always and everywhere," quoted from a Syndicalist handbook written by Charles Watkins, and indorsed by Tom Mann. Vide *The Nineteenth Century*, Sept. 1911, "The Labour Revolt and its Meaning," by J. Ellis Barker.

ism developed in the next stage it brought into clear view the ultimate features of this position.

In syndicalism the controlling factors in the great class war of civilization were defined with firm grasp in the programme set out in 1912 in the leading organ of the movement in England. The demand for the nationalization of industry so prominently displayed in all the earlier pronouncements of socialism was, in that programme, shifted definitely into the background. Syndicalism, it was asserted, had ceased to put its trust in the State. Labour was fighting for its own cause. For syndicalists, it was said, had come to foresee a condition in the future in which the power of the State would be inferior to the power of organized capital, and in which the power of the State under the control of the capitalist would be turned against the workers in an industry that had become nationalized. The universal strike, therefore, to be thoroughly effective in the future must be directed, it was asserted, not simply at curtailing profits. *It must aim to become a menace to the community itself through the stoppage of supplies.*

We have to observe, in short, the labour movement in the West in this phase becoming at last consciously instinct with the principles of universal war resting ultimately on each side on the armed

forces of civilization. This instinct expressed itself
quite clearly in syndicalism in two forms. In one
form it urged the programme of a determined propaganda, addressed to labour by the more moderate
leaders, urging the workers to obtain command of
military force by acquiring as rapidly as possible political control in all the parliaments of the world which
vote supplies for the armed forces of nations. In the
other form the programme became, in the hands of
the more extreme leaders, a propaganda addressed
direct to the soldiers of the nations as the ultimate
units of a civilization in which armies could be turned
against labour in the last arbitrament of war.

In both these positions the leaders of the extreme
wing of labour had come in sight of the situation
which was already actually being discussed by the
leaders of militarism in the military textbooks of
Germany. For in these textbooks the masters of
force had foreseen and had anticipated the day
when, under universal conscription, the soldier himself having become the ultimate unit of civilization
would be subject to " all the tendencies which make
him the child of his time." [1]   The disturbing effect
of such a propaganda as syndicalism contemplated
had indeed haunted the dreams of the masters of

[1] *The German War Book* (*Kriegsbrauch im Landkriege*), J. H.
Morgan's translation.

force. It would, they foresaw, interfere with the efficiency of the instrument of irresistible force which they were forging in civilization. But their policy, in this last resort, had been thought out. It was already outlined in the textbooks of war. It was " to smash the whole fabric of that spiritual life " in the soldier himself,—equally with that of the enemy, for they had counted upon the necessity in both cases,—which ran counter to the policy which demanded success as the supreme object of war.[1]

Thus had the essentially pagan mind of the West reached to the elementals of the atavistic creed of omnipotent force—biological necessity it had become in the military textbooks of Germany—into which it had rendered the thesis which Darwin had given to it fifty years previously.   Slowly but with increasing momentum the curtain was beginning to rise upon the greatest world-drama of force in the history of humanity.

It is necessary to turn now to watch other aspects of this movement in civilization into which all local phases, national and social, have rapidly been

[1] For the teaching as to smashing the spiritual life of the enemy compare *The German War Book* (*Kriegsbrauch im Landkriege*), translated by J. H. Morgan, M.A.   For the teaching as to smashing the spiritual life of the soldier when it ran counter to the necessities of war compare passage quoted from Austrian military textbook, for which and reference see p. 71 of this volume.

drawn. The causes which have driven labour to organization within recent times have been irresistible. But causes operating with a similar intensity have at the same time been driving capital into a position in which all the landmarks of the past are one by one disappearing from view. The enfranchising tendencies in the life of the West have gradually set in motion tidal movements in civilization in which the social emotion is submerging all the fixed points of the past. But there is no indication whatever on the thought or activity of the time that the power-holding interests in civilization have any clear grasp of the situation in which they are involved. We see them rather everywhere falling back instinctively upon positions calculated to give them command in an environment of force if the struggle should resolve itself into one for mastery under more primitive conditions.

In the old individualistic age of the past capitalism had come to rest in large part on the convenient maxims of a science of political economy which identified the operations of capital with the permanent public weal. But the spokesmen of capital have on the whole shown no consciousness that the foundations of this world have moved bodily in our time. As the demand of the proletariat in the modern class war has threatened to become nothing

3

less than the demand for the replacement of capitalism by collectivism supported by the enormous voting power of organized labour, capital has had to face round to meet problems which bring into the front rank of the conflict the most fundamental issues connected with our civilization.

As the spirit of the world fight has gradually enveloped the whole range of the complex activities of the West, the position of capital in relation to the social emotion has assumed features of great interest.   One of the most striking developments of the age has been the colossal concentration of wealth.   Relentlessly driven from two sides towards concentration, from without by labour and from within by the nature of modern enterprise, capital has become aggregated into immense organizations worked on the basis of joint-stock companies.   It has been a peculiar and inherent feature of these aggregations that they have tended through causes which they have been quite unable to control to bring capital profoundly and on a world-wide scale into conflict with the social emotion.

As the leaders of labour with the gathering instinct of the fight strong upon them have sensed the omens of the time in the West, the antagonism to capital has grown rapidly.   In almost every part of the civilized world it has deepened in intensity in the first period of the twentieth century. The case, moreover, which we see being put forward on behalf of the proletariat—a case which is based on the voting power of labour and which orientates itself in the last resort to the armed forces of civilization—has become more uncompromising. It has come to take the form of a determined frontal attack on the whole cause of capitalism.

It amounts, as we see it put forward now, to the arraignment by labour before public opinion of the entire system of modern capitalism on the ground that it is inherently and fundamentally anti-social and therefore impossible. The attack has closely followed the lines I foreshadowed in 1908 in the Herbert Spencer Lecture to the University of Oxford.[1] Everywhere in the struggle we see capital in the West essaying to defend itself on the old lines. The modern tendency to gigantic concentration and control by the few is taken to be a development quite inevitable and in the public good. The circle of shareholders of its joint-stock companies will, it is maintained, become ever wider and wider. Its Companies and its Trusts will tend, therefore, to become at length identified with the general public itself. Its Corporations will tend more and more to become governing industrial republics rest-

[1] *Individualism and After.*

ing on their own representation within the body
politic—a kind of industrial democracy gradually
supplementing and superseding political democracy.

But on the other side we see labour closing for
battle with a vision which it has fixed far beyond
this horizon. It sweeps away almost without
parley the case put against it. The financial republics of joint-stock enterprise, it asserts, have
no counterpart in political democracy. They
manage public utilities on a scale so great that their
affairs are comparable only to the affairs of a first-
class state or a federation of states. But they
outrage the fundamental principles of democracy,
labour asserts, in that they have no relation to
any social or moral principle outside the earning
of dividends ; while they violate the cardinal
necessity of democracy in that voting power is
according to the amount of shares held, and that
control is in the hands of the few who work in the
dark, the vastest returns being obtained by the artificial raising and depressing of the Stock Exchange
value of their securities. Labour does not stay to
argue with the overlords of capital the case for the
wages of capacity in this direction. The gigantic
growth of speculation in Stock Exchange values and
the vast system of finance which accompanies it
have come to be described as parasitic on modern

industry, representing no function that can be expressed in terms of social utility. So the propaganda becomes an appeal for the votes of the proletariat to sweep the whole system away. And the argument, as we have seen, has come in the last resort to envisage without hesitation the ultimate conditions of force and to be consciously addressed to armed men as themselves the ultimate units of civilization.

All these profound movements in the West in which we see the foundations of society being challenged proceed with the same spirit moving through them. We appear to be everywhere witnessing a retreat upon the first principles of war. The *Westminster Gazette*, speaking at the centre of British politics, recently recorded a change in political conditions in Great Britain which a generation ago would have been unthinkable. The journal noted a peculiar fact of our time to consist in the substitution of a condition of uncompromising war resting on violence for a condition of free discussion in all the principal institutions on which popular government rests. The inevitable result, the journal went on to say, is that in parliamentary government the proceedings are becoming " battles rather than deliberations, and that the whole procedure has to be organized on the basis of war . . .

it is now the practice of all minorities to say that they will concede nothing to the majority and to threaten to carry on every controversy by violent and extra-constitutional means." [1]

This is the spirit, the effect of which meets us at every turn in the times in which we are living. We seem to see the male of the West under every form of the activities of civilization enveloped in a kind of monstrous aura of the fight which has become essentially and profoundly atavistic. Speaking of the current life of the West in the year before the outbreak of the great world war, Mr. Harold Begbie asserted: "Look where you will, it is the spirit of I Myself which is paramount. Life exists for Me : all the dim æons behind have toiled to produce Me : This brief moment in the eternal duration of time is only an opportunity for My pleasure and My ease : I care not a jot for the ages ahead and the sons of men who shall inhabit the earth when I am dust beneath their feet. Give Me My Rights. Stand clear of My way. I want and I will have." [2]

The questions which leap into view at this point cannot be avoided. What is the meaning of this tremendous process of life which under all these

[1] *Westminster Gazette*, 30 July 1913.
[2] *The Weakest Link*, p. 43.

aspects in the West is undoubtedly rising to a
climax in history ?   No observer in his senses can
doubt the infinite significance in the world of the
process of enfranchisement, new in the history of
the race, which, moving slowly through long periods
in the past, has brought our civilization to its present
position.   But what is the import of the apparent
rebirth in the West of the pagan mind drunken
with the spirit of force and of that recrudescence of
the forms of force in all the institutions of the
West which in a space of fifty years has followed
the interpretation of the Darwinian thesis of the
world in terms of efficiency resting on force ?   It is
a development which cannot contain the meaning
of the West.   It is a development which is indeed
entirely overshadowed by the significance of another
and counter phenomenon—the ever-rising tide of
the social emotion in our civilization.   For through
all the stress of conflict in the West there swells
the deep diapason of the social passion calling
for service, for subordination, for sacrifice, for
renunciation on a scale unprecedented.   The propaganda which it inspires is, moreover, addressed
no longer to nameless mobs, but through every
avenue of emotion in art and literature to the
minds of voting millions who are themselves the
armed millions and the ultimate units of civiliza-

tion. It is an age of elementals. In the midst of
the rising to the surface again in civilization, on a
scale approaching the universal, of aspects of
savagery belonging to epochs of the past, we are
watching the assembling in the world of the governing forces of new eras of history.

Have the interpreters of Darwinism in the past
missed the great secret of the humanity of the
world? It is becoming evident that all the truth
there is in Darwin's great conception may be summed
up in a single word—integration. For long we have
wasted our breath in talk about the survival of the
fittest and in discussions as to which the fittest
may be. But the fittest in life is simply the most
advanced integration. Darwinism dealt with the
individual and with the individual mostly before
the advent of mind. The law of the integration
of the individual has been the law of the supremacy
and the omnipotence of brute force. But other and
higher integrations are now on foot in the world
which rest on mind and spirit. It is the laws and
the meanings of these integrations which are carrying
the world into new horizons. And in the upbuilding
of the civilization founded on this wider knowledge
it is the stones which the builders of the past have
rejected which are about to become the master
stones of the edifice.

CHAPTER II

THE PSYCHIC CENTRE OF THE GREAT PAGAN RETROGRESSION

WHEN in the autumn of the year 1914 the nations of the world entered almost without warning on the greatest war of all time, in which more than half the human race became engaged, and in which forces numbering considerably more than thirty millions of men met each other armed in the field, the world stood aghast. The magnitude of the conflagration seemed to emphasize in a special manner some gigantic failure of the West in bringing to fruition in history those high expectations of universal peace and goodwill which its leading minds had for centuries held up to humanity. The war was, indeed, an event of far greater significance than any military development that had ever happened in the world. It marked the fact that the climax had been reached in that extraordinary set of conditions described in the last chapter, in which under every phase of its civilization we beheld the West getting down to the first principles of force.

Up to the middle of the nineteenth century, even in the midst of the fiercest, most prolonged and most savage wars, the West had remained consistently steadfast to its conception of civilization as ripening towards a golden age of world peace. The ideal of permanent goodwill among nations and of international arbitration as an ultimate substitute for war had continued to deepen its hold on men's minds during the whole of the period. The Congress of Vienna in 1814-5, at the close of the Napoleonic wars of conquest, although it led to reaction and was a congress of princes rather than of peoples, was held under the influence of visions of a coming age of permanent peace in the world. In 1834 Mazzini and the " Young Europe " association were dreaming of universal fraternity. In 1841 the poet Tennyson, in England, was singing in fervent anticipation of the day when the battle flags of the nations were to be furled in the parliament of man. Through the whole of this decade up to the Saxon revolution in 1848-9 the struggle in progress in most of the central States of Europe was for constitutionalism, and the dreams of their peoples were of lasting peace amongst States and nationalities. A little later many of the foremost minds of civilization were allowing themselves to think with the rulers of Great Britain under the lead of the Prince Consort, that the opening of the Great International Exhibition of 1851 in London marked the practical inauguration of such an era of universal peace.

A change radical and sudden took place soon after 1850 in the spirit of the West. It was a change which did not arise from any causes merely social or political. It was due to forces which were profoundly psychic. It is necessary to understand these forces, for it is in the psychic development which preceded the world war of 1914, that we have to witness the almost incredible spectacle of the entire organized system of that knowledge of the West, which is essentially the science of force, passing gradually to monstrous forms of extravagance and failure, and at length to irretrievable bankruptcy in Western civilization.

By far the most important event in the history of the modern West is that of the publication in 1859 of Darwin's *Origin of Species*. There is no precedent in the history of the human mind to compare with the saturnalia of the Western intellect which followed the publication of this book. Speaking of the event in his Presidential Address to the Royal Society in London in

1905, Sir William Huggins said of the instantaneous revolution it produced : " The accumulated tension burst upon the mind of the whole intelligent world with a suddenness and an overwhelming force for which the strongest material metaphors are poor and inadequate. . . . In a way to which history furnishes no parallel the opinions of mankind may be said to have changed in a day." The change, moreover, produced by the Darwinian hypothesis was not simply one of detail. The revolution seemed to involve the reversal of a position fundamental in Western thought which, to use Sir William Huggins' simile, " like a keystone brought down with it an arch of connected beliefs " that for centuries had formed part of the permanent life inheritance of the civilization of the West.

Darwin's presentation of the evolution of the world as the product of natural selection in never-ceasing war—as a product, that is to say, of a struggle in which the individual efficient in the fight for his own interests was always the winning type—touched the profoundest depths of the psychology of the West. The idea seemed to present the whole order of progress in the world as the result of a purely mechanical and materialistic process resting on force. In so doing it was a conception which reached the springs of that heredity born of the unmeasured ages of conquest out of which the Western mind has come. Within half a century the *Origin of Species* had become the bible of the doctrine of the omnipotence of force.

The hold which the theories of the *Origin of Species* obtained on the popular mind in the West is one of the most remarkable incidents in the history of human thought. The first effect of this presentation of the existing world as the result of selection through struggle and merciless war was immediate. Everywhere throughout civilization an almost inconceivable influence was given to the doctrine of force as the basis of legal authority.

This effect had two deeply marked phases. In countries like England and the United States the striking resemblance which the doctrine of the survival of the fittest in the war for existence bore to those doctrines of political economy which had come to prevail in business and commerce was immediately recognized. Almost every argument of the *Origin of Species* appeared to represent a generalized conception of the effectiveness of the war of competition. The conditions of the social war which Maurice, Ruskin, and a crowd of writers had condemned, but

which Bentham, the Mills, and the influential school
of English utilitarians had long been attempting
to realize in the political State, seemed to have
become justified at a stroke. The central thesis
of Darwin appeared as nothing less than a culminating scientific condemnation of all the labour
programmes of the West conceived in a spirit of
socialism. The prevailing social system, born as it
had been in struggle, and resting as it did in the
last resort on war and on the toil of an excluded
wage-earning proletariat, appeared to have become
clothed with a new and final kind of authority.
Darwinism seemed to the rulers of civilization to
have lifted the veil from life and to have disclosed
to the gaze of the time the self-centred struggle of
the individual ruthlessly pursuing his own interests,
and pursuing them as in the competition of business
to the exclusion of all other conceptions, and to
have revealed this individual as the basal fact of
the world in evolution.

This was the first phase of the effect of Darwin's
conception on civilization. But although Darwinism
was a product of the English-speaking peoples it
was neither in England nor in the United States
that it passed rapidly into the second phase of its
influence. In this phase on the continent of Europe
the extraordinary position was soon reached in

which Darwin's theories came to be openly set out in political and military textbooks as the full justification for war and highly organized schemes of national policy in which the doctrine of Force became the doctrine of Right, and in which force in a manner which had not been known for centuries was openly made the basis of all legal authority.

As the prestige of Darwinism increased and as the new ideas became entrenched in the handbooks of popular science and in systems of revolutionary criticism, it was almost as if the desert and the jungle had begun to voice themselves in human thought. The world beheld the champions of force gradually becoming again in their own right the Supermen of systems of popular philosophy. In solemn treatises of social science it saw them emerging as " efficients." In political science lectures they began to appear as " we who have the Right because we have the Power " of systems of national policy. The doctrine of the supremacy and the omnipotence of force became the doctrine of absolute Right expounded as the law of " biological necessity " in books of state-craft and war-craft, of expanding military empires. And through it all the world saw the " right of conquest " becoming justified and glorified by warlike and military organizations as civilization had never dared to glorify and justify

it before. Soon after the middle of the nineteenth century and onward the history of the West takes on a new
spirit. From this date forward George Peel's terrible
saying that history and homicide are indistinguish-
able terms [1] becomes a truth pregnant with a meaning which it never possessed before in civilization.

To understand clearly the character of this surprising development of which modern Germany
became the life centre in civilization it is necessary
to glance briefly at Darwin's central thesis. The
truth of Darwin's conception may be compressed
within clear boundaries. It is of great importance
to grasp the characteristic outlines thereof. Darwin
gave to the world the true science of the evolution
of the animal in the past epochs of the world. Darwinism is essentially the science of the integration
of the individual efficient in his own interests. " If
A was able to kill B before B killed A, then A survived. And the race became a race of As, inheriting
A's qualities." [2] This was Bagehot's brief and vivid
summary of the Darwinian doctrine. Darwinism is,
in short, the science of the causes which have made
those who are efficient in the struggle for their own
interests supreme and omnipotent in the world.

Now this doctrine has nothing to do with the

---

[1] *The Future of England*, p. 142.
[2] *Physics and Politics*, p. 188.

science of civilization. It is the doctrine of the
efficiency of the animal. It has absolutely nothing
to do with the causes making for collective efficiency
in the social and moral world founded on mind which
is evolving in civilization. Darwinism represents
indeed the very antithesis of the principles of that
social integration which is taking place in civilization. The dividing line, moreover, is absolutely
fundamental. For the first principle of evolution
in the world of the efficient animal of Darwinism
is the supremacy and omnipotence therein of individuals or groups of individuals efficient in their
own interests. The first principle, on the contrary,
in the evolution of the social world of civilization lies
in the subordination of individuals. The ascending
history of the human race is indeed nothing else
than the progressive history of the sacrifice of the
individual efficient for himself to the meaning of
that collective efficiency which is being organized
in civilization gradually merging in the universal.

The progress of humanity has, therefore, over and
above every other feature this meaning. It is the
epic of the vast, tragic, ennobling, immortalizing,
all-conquering ethic of Renunciation. The story of
creation up to and including human savagery is
simply the story of the supremacy in the world of
physical force organized in the life of the efficient

4

individual or the efficient group or the efficient State. But the story of evolution above savagery is nothing else than the story of the gradual rise to supremacy in the world of those psychic forces organized in civilization which are subduing individuals or aggregations of individuals efficient in their own interests to those universal principles which are making for the limitless efficiency of civilization.

It happens through all this that there has never been since civilization began any reconciliation between the morality of the individual efficient for himself and the morality of evolving civilization. There never will be any such reconciliation to the end of time. The two things are inherently incompatible. The meaning which underlies all forms of progress in advanced civilization is that it represents the great spiritual integration of mind which has raised the conception of Right to the plane of the Universal by projecting the sense of human responsibility outside all theories of limited interests whatsoever which rest merely on force. It has made Right independent of and superior to all interests of the individual, the group or the State resting on the successful application of Force, on whatever claim or mission they may be based, on whatever scale they may be represented, by whatever force they may be backed.

The contrary doctrine that Right rests on the successful application of Force in the individual was broken when the day of the highwayman passed in civilization. The organized form of the same doctrines in the State that no Right is above the State, and that the State has no standard but that of "power and expediency"[1] resting on omnipotent force, has been the standing challenge to liberty and progress in every phase of the tremendous struggles which make the history of civilization.

Now if we take up any of the superficial philosophies or false systems of social science of which the world is full, we have the clue at once to their unsoundness. It may be distinguished immediately that they have all one unmistakable mark on them. They represent endeavours to construct the science of evolving humanity without the subordination of the individual to the universal, and therefore without the iron ethic of Renunciation. They are all hopeless attempts foredoomed to failure, to set out the mere science of the animal efficient in his own interests as the science of civilization.

A name may be given to all these sham cults of civilization. They are all essentially pagan. The pagan was originally a villager, the worshipper of

[1] Bernhardi, *Germany and the Next War*, chap. v.

local and therefore of false gods. He was the antithesis of the universal. The modern definition of
paganism may be put clearly and briefly thus :

> The pagan man is the man whose standard of
> Right does not extend beyond his own
> interests.
>
> The pagan state is the state whose standard
> of Right does not extend beyond its own
> interests.

The pagan man and the pagan state may confuse
us at the present day by the profession of exemplary
principles or of exemplary standards of culture
from motives of expediency or opportunism in the
midst of the world by which they are surrounded.
But if they have as part of them no standard of
Right raised to the plane of the Universal and projected outside their interests, they are essentially
pagan. And systems of religion, systems of ethics
and philosophies are all in whole or in part pagan or
the reverse in this sense, as well as men and states.

Now in the light of these facts it is a matter
of peculiar interest to attempt to follow the vast
effort in the life of the modern West to clothe the
ideas of the great pagan retrogression resting on
Darwinism in the language of science and philosophy, and then to embody them in gigantic schemes
of world politics. They all conform to one type.

They all represent historic efforts in one form or
another to present what is essentially Darwin's
science of the individual animal as the science
of civilization. The task is in the nature of things
impossible, for it represents a fundamental confusion of individual efficiency in the animal with
social efficiency in civilization, of the non-moral
with the moral, of the pagan ethics of primitive
man with the advanced ethics of civilization, of the
standards of the jungle with those of evolving
humanity. The elemental extravagances involved
reveal themselves, therefore, at every step, as
almost the whole of civilization is gradually brought
under the influence of these attempts.

It was Prussia first, and then the whole of
Germany, which became the seat of this development. The centre of Darwinism in Germany was
in the writings of Haeckel. But Darwin's theories
and Haeckel's ideas were absorbed and utilized by
a most powerful group of authors and men of action
who, from various standpoints, perceived how
closely the Darwinian doctrines of efficiency re-
sembled the doctrines of efficiency resting on
force, in which they had for long endeavoured to
embody their own conceptions of the national policy
of modern Germany. It was from this intellectual ferment that there gradually spread throughout

civilization a surprising movement the like of which
the human mind will probably never see again.

In watching modern Germany advancing towards
the Armageddon, a psychic centre of particular
interest and significance is in Nietzsche's writings
and in Haeckel's effort to define the ethic of
Darwinism and to compare it with that previously
prevailing in Western civilization. Haeckel's
popularization of Darwin began early, but its
bearing may be best studied in its clearest
form in his *Riddle of the Universe*. In this effort
it may be observed that all the ideas revolve
round a single fundamental conception. According
to Haeckel the supreme mistake of the Christian
ethic consists in this. It conceives that there
exists in the ordinary man a kind of dualism, some
fundamental principle of opposition, that is to say,
between himself and society, between the good of
himself and the good of the world, between the
individual and universal.

According to Haeckel all this is undiluted nonsense. There is no place whatever, he tells us, for
anything of the kind in the Darwinian ethic. Man,
in Haeckel's interpretation of Darwinism, is simply
a " social vertebrate." His social duties and his
duties to himself are, therefore, one and the same,
and grow from the same root in the past. The

whole matter, in short, is that altruism or the good of others " is only enlightened egoism " for the good of oneself.   And " this fundamental law of society, " concludes Haeckel, " is so simple and so inevitable that one cannot understand how it can be contradicted in theory or in practice as is done to-day and has been done for thousands of years." [1]

This is Haeckel's system of monistic ethics. What it represents in reality is the standard of primitive man.   There is naturally and as a matter of course no place in it for that stupendous conflict between limited interests resting on force and the interests of the Universal which forms the main theme of human history.

Thus the categorical imperative of the moral law which demands by an overwhelming instinct the sacrifice of self, and which Kant, therefore, summarizes in the maxim, " Act at all times in suchwise that the act may hold good as a universal law," becomes to Haeckel " Kant's curious idol." [1]   Similarly, the command of the Founder of Christianity, " Love your enemies, bless them that curse you, do good to them that hate you, and pray for them that despitefully use you and persecute you," is pronounced by Haeckel to be " as useless in practice as it is un-

[1] *The Riddle of the Universe*, chap. xix.

natural."[1] And as for the doctrine that "if any
man will take away thy coat let him have thy cloak
also," "what in the light of Darwinism," asks Haeckel
in effect, "could be made of such a doctrine in the
midst of the conditions of the modern world ? "

Haeckel's writings gave to the pagan doctrine
of force an extraordinary prestige in the minds of
the millions who read the popular editions of his
works in Germany, in English-speaking lands, and
in other countries. But Haeckel's attempt to
apply Darwinism to civilization was from the
beginning made in that spirit of compromise which
could not long endure. It was made in that spirit
which distinguished Herbert Spencer's similar
attempt in England, a spirit which has been
described as essentially demoralizing in that it
attempted "to combine the Christian standard of
manners with a materialistic standard of values."[2]
In this it was like the later attempt of the German
General Staff in the *Kriegsbrauch im Landkriege*
so admirably summarized by Professor Morgan
in his translation. It consisted in "laying down
unimpeachable rules (representing the ethic of
civilization) and then destroying them by exceptions (representing the ethic of savagery)."[3]   It was

[1] *The Riddle of the Universe*, chap. xix.
[2] Ford Madox Hueffer, *When Blood is their Argument: an An-
alysis of Prussian Culture*, Pt. II. chap. II. § ii.   [3] *Op. cit.* p. 1.

Nietzsche who flung to the winds all such futile attempts at compromise and who first proclaimed aloud to the world the inner meaning of popular Darwinism, the true ethic of the great pagan revival of the modern West.

The permanent significance of Nietzsche in Western literature springs from a tremendous fact. It is in Nietzsche's writings that the Western mind first beholds laid bare with unspeakable fidelity that overmastering animal soul of the West which represents the individual efficient in the struggle for his own interests, of which Darwin gave us the science. The West was born of force. Its conditions through millenniums of time have been the product of force. All the characteristic science of the West is the organized knowledge of force. Yet the world-shaping tragedy of our times is that the modern West does not stand for the supremacy of force. It represents, on the contrary, that spiritual integration of mind which is making Right superior to force. The modern West represents the doom of the doctrine of force in history. But it is Nietzsche of all the world who has voiced for us the animal soul of the past as it recognizes this terrible issue and as it rages against the meaning of the new world which it feels to be destined to overwhelm it. There is no event in humanity to compare with the drama of the meeting of these two epochs of human evolution in the life of the modern West.

There is not one of us in the dark, efficient, and terrible West who does not feel deep in him the stir of this soul of the past as he watches Nietzsche's tragic spirit go forth in modern literature casting dust to heaven as he curses the advancing armies of progress. There is no foolish and futile effort in Nietzsche as there is in Haeckel to identify his doctrines with the ethic of Christianity, " I impeach the greatest blasphemy in time—the religion which has enchained and softened us." These are Nietzsche's words. And again : "What have we to do with the herd morality which expresses itself in modern democracy ? . . . It is good for cows, women, and Englishmen." He turns, therefore, to voice his soul in the doctrine of the superman— the animal efficient in the struggle for his own interests : " A new table I set over you, oh my brethren. Become hard ; " [1] " For the best things belong to us, the best food, the purest sky, the fairest women, the strongest thoughts. And if men do not give us these things, we take them." [2] Thus do we see the ethic of popular Darwinism passing towards its embodiment in the politics of

[1] *The Twilight of the Idols.*   [2] *Zarathustra.*

the modern State. Thus do we watch it developing into those maxims which applied to the national
policy of modern Germany, come in due time to
carry it to the world developments which began in
the opening days of August 1914.

Nietzsche's teachings represented the interpretation of the popular Darwinism delivered with the
fury and intensity of genius. They fell on unusually
fertile ground in the conditions of modern Germany.
Towards the middle of the nineteenth century the
struggle for constitutionalism was brought to a close
in that country with the collapse of the Saxon
revolution. The policy of Prussia had become the
policy of the sword, and the maxim that "the
destinies of the German people are in the hands
that hold the sword" emerges into open light as
an established principle in the aims of that State.
The incomparable machine of the Prussian army was
used to enforce and to justify the doctrine of force.

Bismarck, in the development of the State policy
of his country, gradually brought into full view in
civilization the working of Nietzsche's conception
that the State founded on successful force is a law
of Right to itself. The idea, inherent in the Darwinian conception of progress, that the main business
of the efficient State is to wage war, came to be
formulated at the same time with increasing clear-

ness and persistence. "We have now agreed," concludes Treitschke in one of his most important lectures, "that war is just and moral, and that the ideal of eternal peace is both unjust and immoral and impossible." [1]

The tendency to exalt, at the expense of society, the absolute claim of the State thus founded on war, went hand in hand with this development. It was put in the most striking manner in a statement quoted from Treitschke : "I have never in my life given one thought to my duties to society ; I have never in my life, by so much as one single thought, neglected to consider my duty to the Prussian State." [2]   The intellect of Germany under the lead of those at the head followed suit and set itself almost as a body to justify and embody in the State, first in Prussia and then in Germany, the Darwinian conception of force.   " The Seminars of the German universities," says Professor Morgan, " were the arsenals that forged the intellectual weapons of the Prussian hegemony.   They all have this in common—that they are merciless to the claims of the small States whose existence seemed to present an obstacle to Prussian aims." [3]

[1] *Treitschke : his Life and Works,* "Essay on International Law."

[2] F. M. Hueffer, *When Blood is their Argument,* Pt. I. chap. iv.

[3] *The German War Book,* translated by J. H. Morgan. Translator's Introduction, chap. iv.

We have to observe in modern Germany, says a recent writer, a grim development, " how professor after professor, whether merely truculent like Treitschke or sedate and comparatively mild-spoken like professors of the school of Ranke and Delbrück, have always come nearer and nearer to the doctrine of force until finally the blinding light of the argument that the first object of the State is the waging of war bursts upon the professorial brain." [1]

It was Darwinism pure and simple, embodied in the State. " If A was able to kill B before B killed A, then A survived. And it would become the destiny of the race to become a race of As inheriting A's qualities." [2] This in actual effect became in large measure the national policy and the national idealism of a great people for two generations in our time. And the theory of Right which accompanied it was simply that those who held the power of the State were not bound by any code of morality save that dictated by the interests of the State thus resting on successful war.

In all these developments the influence of Nietzsche on his time was profound. It exceeded in its own way even the influence of Treitschke's lectures and of Wagner's music. Nationalism, militarism,

---

[1] F. M. Hueffer, *op. cit.*, Pt. I. chap. II. §iv,
[2] Walter Bagehot, *op. cit.*

materialism became the three dominant notes in
the life of modern Germany. After the death of
Bismarck Nietzsche almost took Bismarck's place.
Gradually, as these developments were in progress,
the voices and tendencies which up to the middle
of the nineteenth century had led to the great
democratic movement in the West, and in particular
in Germany, became subdued and muted. Rapidly
from 1860 onward the spirit of the Darwinian
ethic gathered towards ascendancy in the national
politics of Europe. Germany fought Denmark,
Germany fought Austria, Germany fought France.

After 1880 the impulse took on a wider and more
intense world-phase. The Western nations, driven
by the new spirit and in conditions of rivalry in
which they could not help themselves, entered on
the scramble for the world outside of Europe,
engaging in what has been called " the most rapid
and vast career of acquisition that the world had
witnessed since the days of Islam." [1] Within the
two closing decades of the nineteenth century and
the opening decade of the twentieth century the
leading nations of the West in this period of conquest and annexation added to their dominions areas
fifty times as large as that of the United Kingdom.

The spirit underlying these world movements was

[1] George Peel, *The Future of England*, p. 126.

everywhere the same. The development accompanying it was marked by the international phase so accurately described in the quotation given in the previous chapter from the *Westminster Gazette* in which that journal saw the diplomacy of the leading European nations openly reverting to the principles of savagery. The doctrine that Right was ultimately based solely on military strength, and that military power was the supreme test of fitness and efficiency amongst civilized nations, was simultaneously being rapidly developed in textbooks of political and military science in Germany: that the Right of a State turns not on international morality, but " simply and ̗solely on power and expediency " ; [1] that treaties and national engagements ceased to be binding and became " scraps of paper " when they could no longer be supported by the sword, were all the culminating steps by which the doctrine that irresistible force was the sole test of fitness brought the world to the brink of the cataclysm which plunged nine hundred millions of the human race into war in 1914.

The pagan doctrine of force as the supreme test of efficiency in the world which had come out thus naked and unabashed in modern Germany and which was moving towards its organized expression

[1] Bernhardi, *Germany and the Next War*, chap. v.

in national policy had its springs deep down in the tendencies of the intellectual life of every leading Western nation.

There has been nothing in the history of the human mind in the past, there will probably be nothing in the history of the human mind in the future, to compare with the phases of the intellectual movement which in other countries of the West contemporaneously accompanied the phases of the political movement in which the doctrine of the efficient Darwinian animal became embodied in the world policy of modern Germany.

Almost every reading mind of the West which attempted, under the influence of the Darwinian hypothesis, to apply the doctrine of evolution to human society became affected in the same way. Darwin's science of the animal efficient in his own interest was conceived to be the science of civilization itself. In every case the conception gave rise to some monstrous form of extravagance. In the military state in Germany where Darwinism from the beginning took a political direction its culminating phase was found to be in its application to *Weltpolitik*. Nietzsche gave Germany the doctrine of Darwin's efficient animal in the voice of his superman. Bernhardi and the military textbooks in due time gave Germany the doctrine of the superman translated into the national policy of the superstate aiming at world power. Through all the many phases of the movement there ran the same dominating note of intensive self-assertion, the same fundamental conception of the supremacy of force. " Life exists for Me. All the dim æons behind have toiled to produce Me. I am the Fittest. Give Me My Rights. Stand clear of My way. I want and I will have."[1]

All this was in Germany. But in the ultra-democratic State as represented in England, France, and the United States the development of Darwin's ideas took on different but even more surprising forms. In the article on Sociology in the current edition of the *Encyclopædia Britannica* I have dealt with some of these phases. As early as 1860, the year after the publication of Darwin's *Origin of Species*, Herbert Spencer published in England his famous article on the Social Organism. The article contained the central idea around which Spencer afterwards constructed his system of Synthetic Philosophy, the principal books of which have been translated into every leading language of the West.

Nothing has ever existed in the world or will ever exist therein like the social organism which Spencer conceived in this essay. For the characteristic

[1] Harold Begbie, *op. cit.*

5

feature of the social organism of human society, as Spencer described it, was that it is an organism in which the interests of the individuals comprising it can never be subordinated to any supposed interest of the whole. Extraordinary as the fact may seem, this conception is actually put forward by Spencer in all seriousness. It is the leading idea in his system of Synthetic Philosophy. Yet the mind staggers and boggles at the conception. For how could there be such a thing as a social organism while the interests of the individual in it were supreme over every good of the whole organism! Even the arrogance of Nietzsche's superman did not reach that of Spencer's individual as thus conceived.

In ages to come, as men watch the phenomenon of the passing at this time to gigantic catastrophe in history of the whole system of the knowledge of the West which is founded on force, interest will centre in the extraordinary intellectual position thus being developed in England by Spencer side by side with the political development taking place in Germany.

At the time when Spencer wrote the German people were being rapidly enveloped in those theories of the absolute State aiming at world power and resting on militarism which had been placed on the anvil by Frederick the Great of Prussia long before Nietzsche voiced the spirit of these theories, and Haeckel clothed them in the terms of Darwinian science. But Spencer was an Ultra-democrat. He hated militarism. He lived in England. He therefore applied the Darwinian doctrine of the efficient animal in his own way.

Yet the result was essentially identical in both cases. Spencer expressed through the individual challenging with his rights the good of the whole social organism the same Darwinian doctrine of the primitive animal which Haeckel, Bernhardi, and the German General Staff were seeking to embody in the policy of military Germany challenging the world. "The Christian duty of sacrifice for something higher does not exist for the State, for there is nothing higher than it in the world's history," said Bernhardi.[1] "The Christian duty of sacrifice for something higher does not exist for the individual," said Spencer in effect, "for there is nothing higher than the individual in the world's history." It was the same voice. It expressed the same overwhelming intensive self-assertion of the efficient Darwinian animal aiming to be supreme and omnipotent in his own interests. "All the dim æons behind have toiled to produce Me. Give Me My Rights. Stand out of My way. There is nothing in the Universe higher than Me."[2]

[1] *Germany and the Next War*, chap. ii.   [2] Harold Begbie, *op. cit.*

CHAPTER III

THE CULMINATING PHASE OF THE PAGAN ETHIC IN THE WEST

IN England the development of the pagan revival progressed with extreme rapidity, and on every side it continued to give rise to similar phases of extravagance.

Darwin had kept mainly to the purely biological aspect of his own subject. He attempted no comprehensive or systematic study of social affairs or of political society. But in a few chapters of the *Descent of Man* he raised the veil for a moment, sufficient to disclose to the world the true nature of the hopeless impasse towards which that movement in thought receiving its impetus from Darwinism, so forcibly described by Sir William Huggins, was carrying the world.

Now the significance of the true application of the law of natural selection in society consists in this. The first step in understanding what lies beyond Darwinism is to recognize in all its far-reaching import that the human evolution which is proceeding in civilization is a *social*, not an individual integration. The individual of the primitive ages of the race, when A killed B before B was able to kill A, and left his descendants, was the individual efficient in his own interests. He was the individual of whom Darwin gave us the science, of whom Nietzsche's superman gave us the voice, of whom the empire of pagan Rome gave us the culminating stage in history, and of whom the war textbooks of modern Germany gave us some of the maxims revived in terms of the modern military State. But despite these phases the epoch of this individual represents an epoch which is passing out of account in human history. This is the meaning of the modern West. It is the psychic and spiritual forces governing the social integration in which the individual is being subordinated to the universal which have become the winning forces in evolution.

There is not, however, the slightest fore-glimpse of the principles of this wider science of evolution in Darwin. For instance, where in the *Descent of Man* Darwin brings us for a moment into touch with the psychic causes in civilization, he shows no comprehension of the results as the phenomenology of a larger principle of natural selection operating on a higher plane in human society. The subordinating psychic causes which are upbuilding civilization seem simply to bewilder Darwin. He sees them in civilization only as interfering with natural selection—that is to say, with the natural selection of the individual efficient in his own interests. Natural selection, Darwin complained, is tending to become inoperative in civilization. " For," he continued in a surprising passage, " we civilized men do our utmost to check the progress of elimination (of the unfit): we build asylums for the imbeciles, the maimed and the sick ; we institute poor laws, and our medical men exert their utmost skill to save the life of every one to the last moment." [1]

Darwin did not proceed to press to practical issues the conclusions involved in this remarkable and profoundly significant passage. But the effect which such opinions involved of carrying the standards of civilization back to those of primitive man and of eliminating the psychic sense of responsibility to life from its wider function in civilization was evident.

This inevitable effect inherent in Darwinism became more and more pronounced as the militarism of Europe began openly to base itself on the theories of the *Origin of Species*. The reversion to the standards of the jungle as the basis of natural selection in civilization soon became clearly visible in all the literature of the modern military movement in Europe. Thus, in a passage

[1] Darwin, *Descent of Man and Selection in Relation to Sex*, chap. v.

quoted by William James in his *Varieties of Religious Experience*, this standpoint was put with the utmost simplicity in an Austrian military textbook. As the writer viewed the youth of the nations of civilization being called under conscription to the standards of war he says of them : " . . . War and even peace require of the soldier absolutely peculiar standards of morality. The recruit brings with him common moral notions of which he must seek immediately to get rid. For him victory, success, must be *everything* . . . the barbaric tendencies in men come to life again in war, and for war's uses they are incommensurably good." [1]

The same appalling practical logic was put later with more directness in the *Kriegsbrauch im Landkriege*, the textbook issued by the German General Staff for the instruction of German officers. Professor J. H. Morgan in the Introduction to his English translation of the book thus summarizes some of its rules of war in which we see this work of eliminating the psychic sense of human responsibility to life from its higher function in civilization actually being accomplished. " Should they (the peaceful inhabitants of an invaded country) be exposed to the fire of their own troops ? Yes :

---

[1] *Friedens- und Kriegs-moral der Heere.* Quoted by Hamon, *Psychologie du Militaire Professionel*, 1895, p. 41.

it may be indefensible, but its main justification is that it is successful. Should prisoners of war be put to death ? It is always ugly, but it is sometimes expedient. May one hire an assassin, or corrupt a citizen, or incite an incendiary ? Certainly : it may not be reputable and honour may fight shy of it, but the law of war is less touchy. Should the women and children, the old and the feeble, be allowed to depart before a bombardment begins ? On the contrary : their presence is greatly to be desired ; it makes the bombardment all the more effective." [1]

In England all the first attempts to apply the Darwinian conceptions to society were carried along well-marked lines. In the early stages Huxley, Tyndall, Grant Allen, and a crowd of popular writers give currency in England to the applications of Darwinism which Haeckel was voicing in Germany and Renan in France. But the embodiment of the Darwinian theories in the policy of the State did not take place in Great Britain. The movement as a whole reached in England its high-water mark in phases of wider extravagance but all of which preserved their own peculiar characteristics.

[1] *The German War Book : being " The Usages of War on Land,"* issued by the great General Staff of the German Army. Translated by J. H. Morgan, M.A., Professor of Constitutional Law, University College, London, p. 2.

One of the last and greatest of Darwin's contemporaries in Great Britain was Darwin's relative
Sir Francis Galton. In the opening years of the
twentieth century Galton, who in 1907 was my pre-
decessor in delivering the annual Herbert Spencer
Lecture to the University of Oxford, embodied in the
lecture for that year[1] a conception which he had
communicated shortly before to the Sociological
Society in London, for applying Darwinism to the
world on a grand scale. It is a conception which
will assuredly live long in the history of thought.

There is nothing in any literature of the world
quite like this scheme which Galton propounded
for applying the standards of Darwinian efficiency
to humanity. In its own particular way it exceeded
in boldness even that conception developed in
Germany by Clausewitz, Treitschke, Sybel, Von der
Goltz, Bernhardi, and their group, for applying the
standards of the Prussian military caste to civilization. Galton's scheme for improving the world
formed the counterpart from the point of view of
English individualism of that which Treitschke
and Bernhardi desired to achieve through the
methods of the Prussian military State. For what
Galton by his method aimed at, although it was
not a type of the State, was nothing less than the

[1] *Probability, the Foundation of Eugenics.*

scientific breeding on a universal scale of the Nietzschean superman. There have been those who have imagined that the greatest revolution in the history of humanity still lies implicit in Galton's conception—could it only be applied to the world by the methods of the German General Staff!

Galton called his new science Eugenics. Its object, in his own words, was " to deal with all the influences that improve the inborn qualities of the race and develop them to the utmost advantage." [1] The author has as clear a view of his requirements as the German General Staff had of theirs. He found no difficulty whatever with his standards of the best specimens of the race. Even the animals in the Zoological Gardens, he said, might be expected to know the best specimens of their class. This remark was the keynote of the scheme. The best qualities to be bred from would, he intimated, include those such as health, energy, ability, and the like; in particular, the aptitudes required to obtain supremacy in the struggle for success in the various professions and occupations. It was in the purest form the Darwinian science of the selec-

[1] In connection with the research fellowship in the University of London, endowed by Galton in 1904 for the promotion of Eugenics, the subject was defined as " the study of the agencies under social control that may improve or impair the racial qualities of future generations, either physically or mentally."

tion of the individual efficient in the fight for his own interests.   For Galton did not propose to be troubled with any of the difficulties to which codes of ethics had given rise in the past of the world.   He had as short a way with moral standards as the *Kriegsbrauch im Landkriege*.   In the scientific breeding of the race morals, Galton said, would not be considered.   He simply proposed to leave moral standards out of account altogether as involving, to use his own words, " too many hopeless difficulties."

This in all its gaunt simplicity was Galton's proposal. Its object, it will be observed, was the " scientific breeding " of humanity.   Its method was by " the improvement of the inborn qualities " of the race. Almost the first question which comes naturally to the mind to ask on being confronted with a scheme so far-reaching as one for the improved breeding of civilized humanity is : What were Galton's qualifications in putting forward a proposal which went to the roots of every ideal involved in civilization ?

As the result of his earlier observations and researches Galton had been one of the leading upholders previously of that doctrine recently so mercilessly dealt with in the history of the world and now generally discredited, to the effect that the difference between the higher races of civilization and the less developed races of men was one of marked intellectual inferiority on the part of the less developed races. In some of Galton's published researches, as, for instance, those concerning the mental faculties of uncivilized races in South Africa,[1] he went so far as to compare disparagingly the mental faculties of a highly intelligent race like the Demaras with those of the dog. In these researches and subsequent writings Galton seemed to be quite unconscious of the fact that this assumed great intellectual superiority of civilized man over the less developed races had no existence. Like Darwin, Galton had no clear comprehension as to what efficiency in civilization really consists in. He did not see that the superior efficiency of the man of the advanced races was superior *social* efficiency, and that this came to him almost exclusively through the social inheritance, a complex material and psychic inheritance which did not necessitate or indicate anything whatever of the great intellectual superiority which Galton supposed to be inborn in the advanced races.[2]

[1] *Narrative of an Explorer in Tropical South Africa.*

[2] I have dealt with this matter at length in *Social Evolution.* Galton subsequently perceived his original belief, as to the interval between the man of advanced civilization and the savage being mainly one of inborn mental or intellectual difference, to be untenable, but in correspondence, and in conversations I afterwards had with him, I recognized how strongly he remained to the end of his life under the influence of ideas associated with his first conception.

Yet it was Galton, with no higher equipment of knowledge than thus indicated and the subject in the past of so misleading an illusion about a matter so fundamental, who now proposed to enter upon the stupendous task of reconstructing civilization by the scientific breeding of the race ! As might be expected, Galton's conception of civilization in such circumstances was so elementary that there was no place in it for moral standards or for any of those problems of the responsibility of the individual for the universal which have distracted the human mind since the dawn of knowledge and in which centre all the meaning and all the laws of the social integration which humanity is undergoing in civilization.

I was present as one of the members of the Council at the meeting of the Sociological Society, in London, at which Galton first made this scheme public. I remember the day as one of the landmarks of my life. It was the point at which the knowledge first came home to me :

(1) That Darwinism was the sum and flower of the peculiar science of the West, a compound of astonishing learning and incomparable ignorance :

(2) That the characteristic knowledge of the West which had been reduced to science was but the organized form of the doctrine of the supremacy of material force :

(3) That this characteristic science of force could never become the science of civilization : but that as embodied in the West, alike in the military State and in the economic struggle, it was moving through world-shaking catastrophe to irretrievable bankruptcy in history.

There were present at the meeting in London at which Galton read his paper many of the representative men of the time, politicians, publicists, professors of many subjects, doctors of many sciences, authors representing various branches of literature.   The chair was occupied by Professor Karl Pearson, now holding the Professorship of Eugenics, which Galton soon after founded in the University of London.   As I walked out into the Strand from the room in the London School of Economics in which the meeting had been held I well remember the state of my mind.   I found myself looking round in the street for the face of a child to restore me again to the feeling and to the atmosphere of civilization.   For my dominant mental impression was that never before had I been so nearly in touch with the mind and with the standards of primitive man.

It had been rumoured at the meeting that Karl Pearson, who had presided, was to be Galton's intellectual heir in carrying out this Eugenic scheme, and he afterwards accepted the Chair of Eugenics founded at the University. Karl Pearson had been one of the ablest of the group of contemporary evolutionists. To me he had hitherto appeared to have applied the Darwinian hypothesis to carry him to horizons in thought far wider than almost any one of his contemporaries had reached in England. When I arrived home it was with new interest, therefore, that I took down from its shelf his *Ethic of Free Thought*, the book in which most of his boldest ideas had been clothed in the language of science and philosophy.

In the light of Galton's proposals the essays of the book now presented a most remarkable study. I followed the mind of the author through the essays as it rose against the leaders of the great wars of religion of the West, against the spirit of " the seething mass of fanaticism " that the epochs of the past presented to him, against the prejudices, the beliefs, the creeds, the tortures, the butcheries, the blood baths which represented the long struggle of the mind of the terrible pagan West, as it encountered in the integration of the universal world something greater than itself which it understood not. How the author in the name of the intellect stooped over the record, now in sorrow, anon in shame, ever in remote superiority. Yet what an inexplicable spirit appeared to me now to surge through the essays. Despite the immaculate maxims it seemed the voice of Nietzsche's superman. The *Ethic of Free Thought* presented itself to me, as the ethic of *Kriegsbrauch im Landkriege* was afterwards to present itself to Professor Morgan. It laid down unimpeachable rules which represented the ethic of civilization, and then it destroyed them by a spirit and exceptions which represented the ethic of the jungle.

For what did the sum of all the essays in the book amount to? It was expressed perhaps in the clearest terms in the essay entitled the " Moral Basis of Socialism." Professor Pearson urged the claims of his socialist ideal with the fervour of a religious enthusiast. And this was what he conceived the ideal to be. The primary educative mission of modern socialism was, he said, to preach afresh the old conception of the State as it prevailed in ancient Greece. The mind staggered before the atavism of the conception. For has not the whole meaning of the integration which the struggle in Western history has represented for thousands of years consisted in projecting the sense of human responsibility outside the State as it existed in the world of ancient Greece? All the intervening struggle of the ages for the liberty and progress of the world has consisted in making Right independent of and superior to all theories of the political State on whatever claims they may be based, by whatever force they may be backed. Despite the unimpeachable maxims, despite even the outward appeals to the universal and the infinite, I saw the book as the book of the mind of primitive man. I realized it as pagan from cover to cover.

For not only was the apostle of Eugenics in England making exactly the same claim for the ideal embodied in his socialist State that Treitschke, the apostle of militarism, was making for the ideal embodied in the military State in modern Germany. Not only did both ideals represent exactly the same essentially pagan conception of Right identified with a limited absolutism, but each was reared on the same basis of intolerant force. Bernhardi has given the world the ethic of his supreme military State. No one stands above it. Its Might is supreme Right. The whole of its ethic " turns simply and solely on power and expediency." And so also in Karl Pearson's ethic of his socialist State. Our ideal as socialists, he tells us, is this : " Society embodied in the State." No one stood above this State also. For " Socialists," said Karl Pearson, " have to inculcate that spirit which would give

6

offenders against the State short shrift and the nearest lamp-post. Every citizen must learn to say with Louis XIV, 'l'état c'est moi!'"[1] These are his words. Nothing more. From the apostle of Eugenics in his ideal socialist State short shrift and the nearest lamp-post for the offender at the hands of the bystander!

From savagery onwards every excess of the human mind has tended to be surpassed when it brings force to support these limited absolutisms of its own conception. But Karl Pearson seemed to have outbid all precedents, even those of the terrible drama of the Anabaptists of Münster, in his intolerance of offenders against the standards of his own ideal State. Even the zealots of the Inquisition gave the right of trial. Even the lynch law of the backwoods sometimes gave the offender a jury of his peers.

In the passage quoted above, I have given Professor Pearson's exact words. It is necessary thus to repeat them—*ipsissima verba*. For it is not improbable that future generations will find it difficult to believe that such things could be in our time. We can imagine that to those who come after it may appear almost incredible that men could stand in the modern West and, in the name of

[1] *The Ethic of Free Thought*, p. 307.

culture and science, give currency thus to standards and conceptions which represent the childhood of the world and give utterance to them, apparently unforeseeing the bankruptcy and catastrophe in history of the intellectual movement from which they sprang.

As these manifestations of the great pagan movement in the West ran their due course in Great Britain, the incidents of the drama on other sides continued to display the same vast spirit of extravagance. The year before the outbreak of the world war in 1914, the Bishop of Winchester, reviewing the outlook in civilization,[1] emphasized in a striking manner and with a high degree of insight the nature of the principles upon which the characteristic civilization of the West had been based in history. The meaning of the movement which had produced Western civilization the Bishop summarized in a number of principles which may be briefly reduced to two, as follows :—

(1) The gradual assertion in the history of the world of the value, and the equal value, of every human life.

(2) The gradual rise to supremacy in the history of the world of the principle of sacrifice and service over force.

[1] *Presidential Address*, Church Congress, 30 September 1913.

The Bishop of Winchester upheld the ideal inherent in these two movements as a touchstone to distinguish the vitality and permanence of every current social and political development in civilization. It was a true view which represented an accurate summary of the meaning of history, and it embodied roughly in outline the fundamental law of evolution which lies at the base of Western civilization.

When with this fact in mind we turn to the further phases of the Darwinian development the interest deepens as the movement mounts towards its culminating phases. The Herbert Spencer Lecture to the University of Oxford in the year 1912 was delivered by one of the most distinguished of living exponents of biological evolution—namely, Mr. William Bateson, until a short time previously Professor of Biology in the University of Cambridge, and the leader in England of the movement and researches arising out of the Mendelian doctrine of heredity. The title of Mr. Bateson's lecture was *Biological Fact and the Structure of Society*. This lecture possesses a peculiar interest, and its significance for the reasons about to be mentioned exceeds even that of Sir Francis Galton's lecture in the same series just referred to. In Germany the ruling military class had made the Darwinian doctrine of the efficient individual as he existed in primeval times the biological justification of Germany's world policy. It was Bateson who put forward in England the same doctrine as the biological justification for casting the whole set of ideas upon which Western democracy rests upon the rubbish-heap of time.

Down to the time in which we are living a great part had been played in the theories of society of nearly every school of thought in the West by the doctrine of Altruism—that is to say, of the service or the love of others as an evolutionary force in civilization. Mr. Bateson proceeded in this lecture to sweep aside all views of civilization founded on this conception. They were, he said, biologically false. The only instinct, he asserted, which is sufficiently universal to supply the motive for exertion in civilization is the desire to accumulate property in the competitive struggle. Other instincts, among which he puts the altruistic emotions, might, he said, be strongly developed in some. " But," he continues, " they are permanent in very few individuals. They are apt to weaken after adolescence, and to disappear as middle age supervenes." [1]

In the light of this biological generalization Mr. Bateson proceeded with his own remarkable proposals for the improvement and reconstruction of

[1] *Biological Fact and the Structure of Society*, p. 26.

the world.   They were proposals which involved a
direct challenge to the most fundamental of all the
principles associated with the life of Western civilization.   In *Social Evolution* I had previously summarized the central principle of the world development
which the West represented in the phrase *equality
of opportunity*.[1]   The phrase as expressing a clearly
defined and fundamental ideal was immediately
taken into currency in British politics, and soon
after into world politics, being permanently registered as representing an international aim in the
Anglo-Japanese Alliance of 1905.   It was against
this central ideal underlying all forms of social and
political progress in the West for centuries that Mr.
Bateson's challenge was principally directed.

The main proposals in his lecture [2] were in
principle reducible to three, which may be briefly
stated as follows :—

(1) Civilization was not founded on altruism.
The only instinct, Mr. Bateson asserted, which is
sufficiently universal to supply the motive for
civilization, and without which the whole community would slacken and decay, is the desire to
accumulate property.

(2) In civilization so constituted Mr. Bateson

[1] *Social Evolution*, chap. vi. pp. 150–155, etc.
[2] *Biological Fact and the Structure of Society.*

asked for the final rejection of the conception that all men are equal, and of the demand in politics that all men shall have equality of opportunity. For the conception and the demand were, he said, "*founded in natural falsehood.*" [1]

(3) Mr. Bateson asserted, therefore, that in civilization in the future, again to repeat his words, " the aim of social reform must be, not to abolish class, but to provide that each individual shall so far as possible get into the right class and stay there, and usually his children after him." [2]

As we regard these proposals carefully they almost take our breath away. For it will be observed that what Mr. Bateson demanded in the midst of one of the oldest and most influential centres of learning and culture in the West was, in effect, nothing less than the stultification of the characteristic principles which have brought the whole modern world of the civilization of the West into existence. He demanded in particular, it will be observed, the stultification of that fundamental assumption of equality with which the Bishop of Winchester identifies Western progress and which underlies every characteristic demand and programme of Western democracy. The details with which Mr. Bateson supplemented his proposals, such

[1] *Op. cit.*, p. 28.　　　　[2] *Op. cit.*, p. 32.

as Mendelian segregation rising to the sterilization of certain classes of criminals, were all in keeping with the spirit of these two demands.

Now the characteristic mark in history for all time of the modern Prussian school of militarism will be recognized to be this.   Its Professors gradually convinced themselves and then a whole people that the principal business of the State is the making of war.   They took the Darwinian standard of efficiency as it prevailed in the childhood of the world, and boldly applied it to politics and war, imagining this primitive conception to represent the science of efficiency in civilization.   They returned thereby to the standards of the pagan spirit of the West, and made force successfully applied in aggressive war the basis of Right in civilization.   So far all has been clear.

But there was a second and wider conception involved in this doctrine of war as the principal business of the State which Treitschke at first and then the leaders of modern Germany deliberately adopted.   Wars of conquest are but exceptional incidents in the life of civilization.   The second and more significant conception was that it is the economic exploitation of the world under the conditions of modern business and commerce which constitutes the *permanent* conditions of war.

What Mr. Bateson did in effect in these circumstances was to put forward the same biological justification for aggressive war organized in the economic activities of civilization as the Prussian military school did for aggressive war organized in the military activities. And in applying this justification Mr. Bateson proposed to put all the characteristic doctrines of Western democracy on the scrap-heap.

The practical significance of this departure, it will be observed, lay in the proposed application to the world of a more dangerous and more wide-reaching embodiment of the pagan doctrine of Right than any that had ever been made before in history. In the conditions described in the first chapter the world of the West was a hotbed ready to receive this extended doctrine of war. Germany had accepted in full the doctrine that underlying her economic activities was the permanent state of war. But the observer had only to regard the leading political issues in any important country of the West to see that in all countries alike the organization of the world in business and commerce was gradually coming to be treated by all parties as an actual state of war.

It is evident, moreover, that the acceptance by a strong nation of the view that her economic life represented a permanent phase of war was bound to compel other nations to adopt standards in which this fact was recognized.[1]   The same driving necessity began thus to operate in the economic world as in the military world under the phase of universal armaments.   In such circumstances a large and growing section in most of the leading countries in the West had come to regard the external shock of nations in military war as only the last and external phase of the internal form of the economic and social war.

In recent times it was even to be observed how the opposition parties in most countries were ready to accept a modified form of this view.   The dominant note in the programmes of all the popular and progressive parties in the leading countries of the West had come to consist in the standing accusation that governments were the expression of the war of business interests, that it was the warring overlords of business who controlled national resources and international policies,[2] who created public opinion, who made and unmade Governments, who were the real masters of all the resources and affairs of the people.   Modern politics, as the *New York World* put it recently in effect, were

---

[1] I was in close consultation with Mr. Joseph Chamberlain at the period when he abandoned the traditional free trade policy of Great Britain and he often discussed this point of view with me.

[2] Cf. chapters in Mr. J. A. Hobson's *Imperialism*.

becoming the wars of interests carried on through the Government. " Practically all the evils the people are battling with," it continued, " are protected by law and buttressed in government." [1]

It was over this raging battlefield of the underworld of the economic life of the West, the underworld where the idealisms of mind are almost without influence, where all the enfranchising influences of thousands of years of civilization struggle against the deep, massive, primordial instincts of human nature, that Mr. Bateson unfurled his new standard. And the affirmation, which in the name of biological science he proposed to inscribe on it, was that the ruling principle of civilization was not altruism but the desire to possess property ; that the conception that all men are equal must be rejected ; that the demand that all men should have equality of opportunity must be finally refused. For they were all " founded in natural falsehood."

Two years later, before the meeting of the British Association in Australia, Mr. Bateson further developed these views. [2] He saw civilization existing as the result of differentiation transmitted through

[1] Quoted from *New York World* in Continental edition of *Daily Mail*, 19 Jan. 1913.
[2] *Nature*, 20 and 27 August 1914.

individual heredity. His ideal was, therefore, the revival in civilization of a kind of hereditary caste system in which every member of society should be got into his right class and should stay there. The methods of government in this eugenic civilization were apparently to be almost as drastic as in Professor Pearson's ideal socialist State. Mr. Bateson proposed to begin comparatively mildly with the feeble-minded. To use his words, "The union of such social vermin we should no more permit than we should allow parasites to breed on our own bodies." [1]

It was an astounding spectacle. The absolute unconsciousness in the mind of the man of science of the part played by the psychic forces in the evolution of society and of the causes of efficiency in civilization could hardly be more strikingly marked. Mr. Bateson abolished with a stroke not only the principles of Western civilization—the sense of responsibility to life, the value, and the equal value, of every human life—as they were set out by the Bishop of Winchester. He proceeded, in the frame of mind in which he was able to speak of a class of his fellow-creatures as " social vermin," to wipe out the very spirit of that sense of responsibility to life which had created the ethos of the Western world,

[1] *Nature*, 27 August 1914.

which was gradually raising the mind of the West to the plane of the universal, and which lay behind all the influence of the liberating ideals of Western civilization upon humanity.

The mind struggles for a time with the train of ideas which are suggested. But in this case also it is the picture of the childhood of the world which at last holds it against other conceptions. On reading through these lectures of Mr. Bateson it is almost as if we saw in imagination the primitive man of past æons of time presenting himself before a congress of civilization, holding again a dripping head in one hand and an ensanguined spear in the other, and, entirely unconscious of the meaning of all the vast struggles for human liberties, demanding in the name of science the restitution of that primal law of the jungle by which the fittest to secure property in the fight survived and transmitted his qualities, all subsequent social conditions being denounced as " founded in natural falsehood."

Mr. Bateson was President of the British Association for the Advancement of Science at its session for the year 1914 held in Australia. It was a fitting climax which awaited this surprising phase in the history of the Western mind. When Mr. Bateson and the British Association left England in the summer of 1914 the world was in a state of armed peace. Before they reached Australia the Armageddon was upon the nations, and the rulers of the German people and the German Military Staff were in the midst of the practical application in the national policy of their country of the ideas and principles discussed in this chapter. They had embarked in that great experiment in the science of social efficiency spoken of by Huxley, where the subjects are peoples and types of civilization, but where all deductions and verifications come too late, and are only in time to be embodied in great systems of history, of morality, and of religion.[1] It was a personal part of this vast climax that Mr. Bateson should return to his native country in a ship continuously in fear of the acts of the war in progress, a war soon to be developed by Germany along the lines defined and defended in the *Kriegsbrauch im Landkriege* into a policy which was to shock, astonish, and awe the world of civilization.

In following the great pagan revival in the history of the Western intellect as here described the mind feels that it indicates that kind of preliminary elemental phase which separates two epochs of evolution. It is impossible to believe that the doctrines discussed in this chapter, put forward in the name of science under so many different phases in

[1] J. H. Huxley, *Lay Sermons.*

the activities of the West, but always with essentially the same meaning under all the forms, have any permanent place of authority in evolving civilization.

" Western Science," said P. Ramanathan, Solicitor-General of Ceylon, speaking some years ago of its teaching in relation to the causes of efficiency in civilization, " is ignorant knowledge." [1] It was a saying so daring that the Western mind merely passed it by. But it is a saying likely to arrest the thought of the West long into the future.

The revolutionary changes that have taken place in recent times have left the essentially pagan and unimaginative mind of the West in a state of indescribable collapse as regards its higher faculties. The fighting male of the West, the product of war long before history has account of him, has turned in our time, bored beyond the last degree of sustenance, from all the problems of the intellect. From the blasphemies of his superman; from those sterile quests after the nature of the Absolute which represent the exhausted residuum of mediævalism; from the hopeless efforts of the intellect to hold the mind of youth at our centres of learning in the West like those displayed in the appalling records of the Moral Science Tripos for the last two generations at Cambridge University, England; from the

[1] " The Miscarriage of Life in the West," *Hibbert Journal, 7. 1.*

cynicisms, the nihilisms, the paradoxes of our schools of intellectual criticism; from the vast libraries created in the name of culture, mausoleums, houses of the dead, accumulations of books for which there are no readers, to use Lord Rosebery's description; from the futilities of Eugenics, ignorantly endeavouring to construct a science of civilization out of the Darwinism of the animal; from the sociology of the schools moved to profound depths of scholarship over the significance of totemism or the rites associated with the age of puberty in the savage maiden while remaining utterly unconscious of the significance of the psychic forces expressing themselves in the great systems of emotion and idealism, the social meaning of which envelops the planet; from the gigantic problems of his Trusts and Corporations with their systems of graft and scandals on one continent; from the equally gigantic problems of his proletariat on another; and then again from the problems of all the races which he has alternately endeavoured to enslave, to exploit, and to enfranchise in the other continents of the world; from the Churches which have filled the world with wars of dogma while remaining unconscious of the greatest dogma of all, that the system of truth which has superseded paganism has its living credentials in its meaning

as the science of civilization—from all these the
essential pagan of the West turned in our time to
the gross unimaginative materialism of military and
economic war.

But with the sense of his coming bankruptcy
upon him the moods of atavism in the pagan of the
West are like the moods of Saul. In one phase he
is the being who has created the hell of the Armageddon. In another he is maudlin with the pity
of reaction and babbles of beating his swords into
ploughshares. In one phase he is emancipating
his womankind, representing half the population of
the earth, from the effects of the ages of the rule of
brute force upon her. In another the savageries of
his Schopenhauers, his Nietzsches, and his Weinigers
towards her awake in his soul the fierce animal
delirium of the jungle. In one hemisphere he wags
his head sentimentally to the chorus of Tannhäuser.
In another the echoes of his rag-time music move
him to shuddering ecstasy as he hears in them the
iron clang of the mills of force in the world he has
created. In one phase his adventurers accumulate
private fortunes in commerce and industry so vast
that they are reckoned in tens of millions of pounds,
so power compelling that they throw those of the
age of Marcus Licinius Crassus into insignificance.
In another the chief medical officer of the governing

7

body of the largest and richest city in civilization reports that of the 172,619 school-children examined by him in a single year one-half were suffering from some definite organic defect " resulting from sheer poverty." [1]   In one phase he is the champion of his civilization as the universal triumph of mind and enlightenment.   In another, in the highest intellectual nation of the West, the silent verdict of the people on the conditions in which they lived at the outbreak of the world war of 1914 was that they had gradually ceased to bring into being as many children as were necessary to the community.

[1] Annual Report, 1910 (London County Council).   Cf. *Times,* 2 April 1912.

PART II

THE BASIS OF INTEGRATING POWER

CHAPTER IV

POWER IN CIVILIZATION RESTS ON COLLECTIVE EMOTION, NOT ON REASON

IN setting out to write the chapters in this section and those which follow, I feel that I am engaging in the presentation in brief outline of the system of knowledge which must in the order of nature become the basis of a new type of civilization. The reason for this conviction will appear presently; but it is desirable at this point to endeavour to get as clear and firm a grasp as possible of a few fundamental positions which are involved at the outset.

It will have been noticed in the preceding chapters dealing with the failure of Western knowledge that all the leaders of the great pagan revival in the West have given prominence to one leading idea, namely, that of inborn heredity as the basis of the fabric of civilization. For over half a century this idea has been put forward with great force as the direct opposite of two conceptions previously deeply entrenched in the life of the West and both

inherent in the Christian system of ethics.   The
first was the conception of the equality of all men,
fundamental alike in the Christian religion and in
all the ideals of the democratic movement in
Western history.   The second was the conception
that the mind of the child in each generation is
like a blank page upon which good or evil training
produces indelible results, this being also a root
conception of Christian ethics.

To both these ideas, basal in Western thought
for centuries, the science which Darwin expounded ran directly counter.   It was based
on struggle resting on inequality.   It centred in
inborn heredity.   If in the struggle for existence
A was able to kill B before B killed A, then the
race became a race of As inheriting A's qualities.
This was the Darwinian science of evolution in brief.
It was based on inborn heredity.   There is, accordingly, no idea more in prominence in all those modern
phases of Western science in which the endeavour
has been to make the Darwinian hypothesis the
basis of a science of civilization than the conception of the dominant influence of inborn heredity.

It may be noticed how this idea of a fixed and
almost unchangeable heredity for the races and
peoples included in civilization has come in our time
to colour nearly all political and social theories in

the West. Writers in the newspapers and reviews of the day continually give it great prominence. In Great Britain and America, since Herbert Spencer's social theories began to affect opinion, those sharing his views have been strongly under the influence of the idea of inborn heredity as the controlling factor in civilization. On the continent of Europe the conception of Darwinian heredity has formed the basis of nearly all modern theories about the relations of the individual to society. Haeckel made heredity the foundation of his ethics. Lombroso and his school made heredity the basis of their characteristic theories about individual faculties in their relation to society. The group of writers on political science which most profoundly influenced the development of modern Germany in the period before the Great War which opened in 1914 were deeply influenced by the idea of heredity. Bernhardi in his pages continually glorifies in Darwinian terms the characteristic fighting heredity of the West. Even Treitschke's essays are strewn with expressions such as "noble nations," "brave races," and with references to the physical and mental inheritance of the Germanic and other peoples, all of which, like most of the Darwinian theories quoted by Bernhardi, imply this conception of the overruling importance of inborn heredity.

The idea that civilization is based on fixed and permanent heredity in the individual has been in recent times in a special sense an overwhelming prepossession with that large group of modern writers in all Western lands who have attempted to apply pure biological conceptions to theories of civilization. The assumption that civilization rests on a great intellectual superiority, imagined as inborn in civilized man as contrasted with the savage, was the fundamental preoccupation of Galton's mind in his discussion of the difference between men of the advanced and the less advanced races. It was the assumption of a corresponding great intellectual inferiority inborn in uncivilized man which led him to his notorious comparison of the mental traits of the Demara race with those of his dog, in which he told us that taking the two, the dog and the Demara, " the comparison reflected no great honour on the man." [1]   In all his eugenic imaginings Galton remained strongly under the influence of this conception of inborn heredity.

Bateson similarly may be seen to have his mind fixed in the same direction in his dream of civilization relapsing into a kind of caste system, founded upon inborn faculties. Bagehot had a conception of inborn heredity permanently in view in his

[1] *Narrative of an Explorer in Tropical South Africa.*

theories of politics. Karl Pearson, whose horizon is wider than that of Galton, may be distinguished to be always more or less under the influence of the same idea of the slow change and comparative permanence of type in human society. The man of the study and of the laboratory, whom he considers to be the proper judge in these matters, knows full well, Pearson tells us, that human society cannot be changed in a year, scarcely in a hundred years ; for it is controlled, he points out, by laws of psychological influence such as temperament, impulse, and passion relatively so unchangeable in their direction that " no single man, no single group of men, no generation of men, can remodel human society." [1]

Now one of the first steps necessary for a true conception of the forces controlling civilization and, therefore, to a true conception of the possibility of an entirely new order of civilization, is to understand that most of these assumptions about inborn heredity as the basis of civilization have no foundation in fact. They are, on the contrary, directly in the face of incontrovertible facts of quite a different significance. The increasing interval between civilization and savagery does not depend upon inborn heredity. The science of

[1] *The Ethic of Free Thought,* v.

civilization has almost nothing to do with the facts of inborn heredity. So far from civilization being practically unchangeable or only changeable through influences operating slowly over long periods of time, the world can be changed in a brief space of time. Within the life of a single generation it can be made to undergo changes so profound, so revolutionary, so permanent, that it would almost appear as if human nature itself had been completely altered in the interval.

The mechanism and the forces, moreover, capable of producing changes of this nature already exist in the world. They are to be witnessed at work on every side of us. The science of the organization of this mechanism and of the control of these forces is the real science of civilization. It represents, at present, an almost unexplored world of knowledge. If but one-half the intelligence and effort which nations have hitherto directed towards the collective organization of society for war were directed towards the study and collective organization of society in the light of this knowledge, it would result in it becoming visible on all hands that civilization can be altered so radically and so quickly that the outlook of humanity on nearly every fundamental matter can be changed in a single generation.

Let us see if we can grasp the first outlines of a position the complete understanding of which will within a short space in the future be perceived to have become the first necessity of all governments, of all reformers, and of all masters of force in civilization. The mechanism by which limitless and transforming power is capable of being almost suddenly embodied in advancing civilization is absolutely different from that mechanism with which, until quite recently, it was the almost universal custom of the world to believe that human progress was associated.

Germany has been the first country of the West to bring home to the minds of men, though unfortunately only in relation to the atavisms of war, the fact nevertheless indisputable and of the very highest significance to civilization, that an entire nation may be completely altered in character, in outlook, and in motive in a single generation. A great number of recent books deal with the subject from various points of view. But nearly all the writers agree in the absolutely fundamental and universal nature of the change which was accomplished on a whole nation in a brief period. This vast transformation of a people was practically achieved in some twenty years, says a writer of experience.[1]

[1] Charles Tower, *Changing Germany.*

It was accomplished so thoroughly, says another well - informed writer, that almost everything previously included in the type of " German " disappeared within a few decades. The alteration which took place in the psychology of the German peoples the writer describes to be a phenomenon so vast and so powerful that it permanently influenced the human mind, while it has been on such a scale that there is nothing to compare with it in history.[1]

The suddenness even more than the completeness of the change is a fact to arrest attention even in the least observant. Most private persons with any considerable experience of Germany and the German people will have been struck with this feature. One of the closest friends of my youth for many years was a retired captain of the German navy, whose type of mind, ideas, and motives appeared to me from practical contact with his surroundings in his own country to be quite usual among the educated classes in Germany in the days when he grew to manhood. In the uprising generation of the German nation of sixty-five millions there is probably not a single individual of this type now in existence. The alteration was not principally a change in individuals in relation to

[1] Cf. F. M. Hueffer, *When Blood is their Argument*, Pts. II. and III.

their interests. It was a change so profoundly and dynamically affecting the entire German nation in its attitude to the world that it has already influenced to an incalculable degree the history of civilization.

All this, it must be remembered, was accomplished by a ruling class in Germany almost exclusively in pursuit of those ideals of war described in the previous chapter. But, quite apart from the nature of the ideals involved in the change, it is the fact of the change itself, its thoroughness, its completeness, its universality, and its suddenness, which are to be noted here as a phenomenon of an importance of the very first order.

A revolution of a different character which has taken place under similar circumstances in the psychology of another nation in almost as brief a period is even more remarkable. In the Japanese people the West has beheld an Eastern nation within the space of less than two generations pass through the whole interval which separates feudalism from modern conditions. In this space of time, a change in general habits, in social and mental outlook, and in national consciousness, was accomplished as by the wand of a conjurer. The new social inheritance thus almost suddenly acquired has been so transforming in its effects and has so powerfully affected the potentiality of Japan in the world that in the brief period mentioned results have been attained absolutely in the face of all that was previously believed to be possible.

Civilization has seen a people formerly negligible and regarded as unfit for association with Western nations attaining almost at a bound an efficiency in the arts of peace and later in the stern stress of war which has given them a place of equality as a great power amongst the leading nations of civilization. By collectively submitting themselves with full intent to a new kind of social inheritance the Japanese people attained in less than two generations to a position which it has taken the principal Occidental nations centuries of stress to reach in the ordinary process of development.

The historian of the future, looking back, will perceive that for three centuries there have been no events in the world to compare in significance and in the lessons which they bear for the future with this sudden transformation of modern Japan and modern Germany. A new science, a new order of ideas, a new kind of knowledge of which the very elements are still almost unknown has come within the vision of civilization.

Some years ago, when I published in *Social Evolution* a destructive criticism of Galton's examination of the mental faculties of members of what he imagined to be the lower races, it came as a kind of revelation to a large number of minds and even to many minds scientifically trained to learn that there existed no wide inborn interval of superiority, intellectual or mental, between even the foremost races of civilized men and the savage. The efficiency which civilization possessed over savagery rested, I asserted, on a basis quite other than that which had been hitherto almost universally assumed.

It was in this connexion that I put on record at the time a prediction which must now be referred to.[1] I ventured then to assert that sooner or later it would become clear in the actual stress of the world, that the Western peoples in basing a claim to supremacy on the assumption that they possessed any inborn intellectual or other mental superiority over the less advanced races of men, were building on a false hope. All the promise of the intellect in the past in this respect was destined, I foretold, to end in disillusionment. Civilization rested, it was asserted, not on the intellect or on the reasoning processes of mind, but on the psychic inheritance transmitted from generation to generation and entirely independent of inborn heredity in the

[1] *Social Evolution*, chap. ix. p. 244 and following.

individual. All that part of the inheritance of civilization which consisted of the conquests of the intellect and of the arts, sciences, and other products of mind would, I asserted, be rapidly acquired by the less advanced peoples and would in the future be utilized with surprising effect against the most developed races by peoples upon whom they had previously looked down.

This prediction has been literally fulfilled in the world since I wrote it. It was made over twenty years ago, not only before the recent Russo-Japanese War, but before the war between Japan and China which preceded it, and at a period when no Western power had yet dreamed of Japan obtaining admission to the circle of the great powers of the world in virtue of her own proved military efficiency displayed through the acquired art and methods of Western war. All the science of expanding civilization in the future is related to the as yet unexplored principles underlying the changes thus almost suddenly effected in the recent history of Japan, and in the surprising history of modern Germany. We have touched therein only the fringe of a vast subject, and this only in one phase of it.

It is necessary to get a grasp of the physical basis of the process in human nature underlying these events before the reach of it in the future of civilization can be fully distinguished. A zoologist in the front rank who has carried the purely biological phase of this subject furthest since I wrote is Sir Edwin Ray Lankester, F.R.S. In the article on Zoology in the current edition of the *Encyclopædia Britannica* this writer has recently remarked with great emphasis on the significance to civilization of the mechanism of that kind of social inheritance which I described in *Social Evolution*.

Sir Edwin Ray Lankester describes the main fact with which it is concerned as "a new and unprecedented factor in organic development." All inquiry in the past has been, he asserts, dominated by erroneous ideas. The heredity with which civilization is supremely concerned is not that which is inborn in the individual. It is the social inheritance which constitutes the dominant factor in human progress, this kind of heredity being, to use Sir Edwin Ray Lankester's words, "completely free from the limitations of protoplasmic continuity. . . . It grows and develops," he continues, "by laws other than those affecting the perishable bodies of successive generations of mankind," so that in every generation the child has to begin with, as it were, a clean slate, the inheritance thus conveyed exercising "an incomparable influence on the educable brain."

8

It must always be remembered there is not inborn in any one of us any part of the effects either of the good or of the evil of this collective heredity, including its psychic elements. If it were interrupted, therefore, in the case of society and the inheritance was not thus conveyed between any two generations either by teaching or by imitation, the result would be extraordinary. There would be a sudden breach in the whole order of civilization. Men would be born mentally and physically the same, but they would inherit in themselves no trace and none of the effects of the past knowledge or training of society,

This impressive fact is to some extent already dimly apprehended by the general mind through the bearings of it being constantly brought under notice by systems of education. But the contrary fact has never been grasped by the human mind in all its significance. *If the incoming generation of men were submitted to a new collective inheritance, including in particular its psychic elements, they would take it up as readily as they did the old. We should then have the surprising spectacle of a great change in the world, appearing to the observer as if a fundamental alteration in human nature had suddenly taken place on a universal scale.*

It is to this fact more than to any other in the

entire domain of human knowledge that the science
of civilization is fundamentally related. All facts
and theories concerned with the inborn qualities of
individuals have an entirely minor significance in
comparison. To obtain control of the mechanism
of this collective heredity which, as we shall see
presently, is principally psychic in its main elements,
is the coming problem of civilization over which
the mind of the world will be engaged for long into
the future.

Now the immense potentiality of this collective
heredity as the cause of efficiency in civilization
is due to two things, one of which carries us considerably beyond the extended horizon of Sir Edwin
Ray Lankester's striking outlook. It is due, in the
first place, to that accumulation of recorded knowledge in the social inheritance which this writer
had mainly in view. But it is due, in the second
place, and far more distinctly, to the creation and
transmission as part of the collective heredity of that
psychic element which consists of ideas and idealisms
that rest on emotion, and which are conveyed to
the young under the influence of psychic emotion.
These have a different physical basis in human
nature from the laws of the reasoning process of
mind with which the textbooks of the West have
hitherto been mainly filled. But this psychic

inheritance in civilization is the most influential of all elements in the collective heredity. The importance of it is profound, and far exceeds that of inborn heredity in the individual. It is capable of bringing into existence orders of men permanently endowed with characters, feelings, standards of conduct from the influence of which they can never free themselves, and the distinctive mark of which is the power of renunciation and sacrifice which they create in the individual.

In the future it will be seen clearly that all Western knowledge is passing in our time through a profound revolution. In the past the Western intellect has been exclusively concentrated on that phenomenon in time which may be described as the emergence of the efficient individual. The science of this efficient individual is founded on Reason. Reason is essentially the knowledge of material force and not the knowledge of the world as it is. It is the far-flung science, that is to say, of the causes which enabled A to kill B before B was able to kill A in the environment which has prevailed in the past of the world. The higher controversies in Western knowledge for half a century past, in which minds like those of Bergson, Bradley, James, Balfour, Ward, Schiller, Lange, Lodge, McTaggart, Tolstoy, McDougall, and a multitude of others have taken part, have one clue that runs through all the various positions developed therein. They all represent that phase of modern thought in the West in which the effort is being made to separate the psychology of the individual integration from the psychology of the social integration, this last merging in the universal and the infinite.[1]   It is with the laws of the integration of the individual efficient in the struggle for his own interests that nearly all the scientific textbooks of the West have hitherto been filled.   From physiology to ethics, from economics and political science to psychology, this is so.   *All this system of knowledge is passing to the rubbish-heap of time as the science of civilization.*

It is in the social integration that man must reach his highest efficiency.   The laws of the social integration are psychic in character, and they must in the nature of things control the evolution of the human mind and all its contents.   The laws of social emotion, as Dr. A. Sutherland[2] was the first clearly to indicate, have a different physical basis in the human organism from the laws of mind which express themselves in Reason. The cause of human progress is psychic emotion.

[1] This has been the most striking fact in evidence in the pages of periodicals like *Mind* and the *Hibbert Journal* for a considerable period.

[2] *Origin of the Moral Instincts.*

The great secret of the coming age of the world is that civilization rests not on Reason but on Emotion.

One of the most remarkable results of the concentration of the Western mind for ages on the phenomenon of the emergence of the individual efficient in his own interests just referred to is our position in relation to emotion. We know of emotion mainly only as related to the science of this efficient animal. In civilization we are constantly under the necessity of controlling this kind of emotion in the daily conflict of life. But it has followed as one of the consequences resulting from this that a considerable part, even of the educated world, has acquired the habit of conceiving a restricted capacity for emotion to be a feature of advancing civilization. The mistake arises from a fundamental confusion of ideas. It is the *control* of emotion, not the absence of it, which is the mark of high civilization. *Other things being equal, the higher and more complete the individual or the people, the higher and more complete the capacity for emotion.*

In civilization as it exists around us at present there is visible on every hand the influence of this element of psychic emotion transmitted in the collective inheritance. We get phases of it in the deep effects of national training and national ethics on different peoples, directed in the past almost solely to the realization of the ideals of war. It is visible in the influence of ideas, and of standards of opinion on classes, groups, and unions of men. But the most striking and permanent results of psychic emotion thus transmitted in civilization are visible in the intensive culture of mind and spirit which forms of belief, and especially the higher types of religion, are capable of producing on men and peoples.

With the single exception of gigantic effort devoted to the national ideal of sacrifice in the cause of successful war, of which the results in recent history have been astounding, the world has witnessed no example in its history of the idealisms of mind universally imposed through intensive culture on the youth of civilization in conditions of emotion and with all the equipment and resources of modern civilization in the background. The great systems of religion which have come nearest to realizing such a conception in the past have not so far even remotely approached what is possible under modern conditions of knowledge. We are on the verge of a new era of civilization, and the people or the type of civilization which will first succeed in this experiment will obtain control of all the reservoirs of force in civilization in a manner which has never been thought possible in the past.

There is not an existing institution in the world of civilized humanity which cannot be profoundly modified or altered, or abolished in a generation. There is no form or order of government or of the dominion of force which cannot be removed out of the world within a generation. There is no ideal in conformity with the principles of civilization dreamed of by any dreamer or idealist which cannot be realized within the lifetime of those around him. Treitschke, as a young university lecturer, speaking in 1863, was prophesying further and truer than he knew when he said there was no ideal which a living people chose to put before themselves that they had not the power of realizing in history.[1] If only the German people had been free to embody this teaching in an ideal of civilization, what might not modern Germany have accomplished in the world !

[1] Adolf Hausrath, *Life of Treitschke.*

CHAPTER V

THE EMOTION OF THE IDEAL IS THE SUPREME PRINCIPLE OF EFFICIENCY IN THE COLLECTIVE STRUGGLE OF THE WORLD

TO get outside the effects of the obsessions of the past, and to be able to look the world straight in the face as it exists, is to have the conviction take possession of the mind with overwhelming force that the civilization of the West is as yet scarcely more than glorified savagery. What has happened in it is that those who have obtained power have endeavoured in the main to found all Western institutions on the heredity of the individual efficient in the struggle for his own interests. Taking this inborn heredity coming straight down from the time when the universal effort was for A to kill B before B was able to kill A, those who have prevailed thereby have organized it into what is called civilization. The result has been inevitable. In our international relations, to use the Hon. George Peel's memorable phrase, Western history is synonymous with universal homicide. And as the scales fall from our eyes we see our economic systems driven by the same inherent heredity, not indeed clothed in the euphemisms with which our textbooks have sought to robe them, but naked, and rather, as Treitschke described them, the permanent types of this business of war in which men stand continuously facing each other.

Civilization, in short, has not arrived. The characteristic power of civilization which renders it irresistible has never been brought into action. The stupendous potentiality of civilization as distinct from barbarism consists in its cultural or collective heredity imposed on the rising generation under suitable conditions. The most important element in this, namely, the idealisms of mind and spirit conveyed to the young of each generation under the influence of the social passion, is absolutely limitless in its effect. The power which is represented thereby is capable of creating a new world in the lifetime of a generation. It is capable of sweeping away in a single generation any existing order of the world. But it has never been seen actually in being, directed and controlled by civilization.

The recent fitful example of the reach of this power in the astounding history of modern Germany is the greatest event in modern history. But it is an event in which we have but the record of the creation and the use of cultural heredity directed almost exclusively to the ends of war, and to the fastening on the world of ideals founded on war, and dependent on war for their maintenance. Even so directed it has produced an example in history of organized self-sacrifice so colossal and so admirable as to appear, to use the words of a recent American writer, "almost superhuman," albeit an example of almost superhuman power so misdirected as to constitute ", one of the most pathetic events in the history of mankind." [1]

It is impossible to believe that civilization will allow the limitless power which it thus possesses to continue to be misdirected in this manner or to continue to lie latent. The endeavour to impose the idealisms of civilization collectively on the mind of the rising generation on an immense scale, with deliberation and intent, and with all the machinery of high organization under conditions in which the social emotion is profoundly moved is bound to be made in the future on a great scale.

The processes of the age have become a machinery for presenting the idealisms of mind to the general imagination with a hypnotic effect never before possible. The significance of the new forces has

[1] " From an American," *Times*, 11 June 1915.

naturally been felt first and most deeply at the great centres of the nervous system of civilization represented by the national life of the leading countries. But this significance extends far beyond its relation to the ideals of nationality. Every institution in civilization is in fore-grips with a new kind of knowledge, the control of which will become a matter of life and death to it. It is clearly in evidence that the science of creating and transmitting public opinion under the influence of collective emotion is about to become the principal science of civilization to the mastery of which all governments and all powerful interests will in the future address themselves with every resource at their command.

It represents an enormous advance in knowledge once to grasp firmly in all its far-reaching import the fact that the human faculty in which centres the integration that is taking place in civilization is not the reasoning process of mind but *the emotion of the ideal*. At no distant time it will be seen that all the principal movements in Western thought since I published *Social Evolution* represent the ever-widening adjustment to this fact of the old intellectual positions. Whether we watch at our centres of learning writers like Mr. F. C. S. Schiller declaring the reasoned quest after absolute truth to be no longer an operative ideal,[1] or Bergson describing the characteristic force of the world as that driving man to extract from himself more than there is by actual creation,[2] or William James declaring that it is absolutely hopeless to attempt to demonstrate by purely intellectual processes the nature of the inner life in us which is nevertheless creating the world,[3] the reach and significance of the process of change is apparent.

The immature imaginings of the past about the place of reason in the world will all in time be put aside. Reason, whether it weighs the planets or discusses the nature of the Absolute, is but the mechanism of mind evolved in the past in correspondence to those forces which produced the *individual integration*. The individual of the past has of necessity been the individual efficient in the struggle for his own interests. But in the *social integration* which is proceeding, the eternal law of efficiency cannot be stated in terms of reason. For it can only be summarized in one word—Sacrifice.

In this stage the law of efficiency is always sacrifice —that sacrifice of the unit, the capacity for which in man proceeds from the emotion of the ideal

---

[1] " Infallibility and Toleration," *Hibbert Journal*, 7. 1.

[2] *Hibbert Journal*, October 1911.

[3] *The Varieties of Religious Experience.*

alone. The power of sacrifice and renunciation is the first and last word in that kind of efficiency which is deepening in the social era of the race. Man can only reach his highest power in the social integration ; and there is no cause in the universe which is able to render the individual, who is efficient in the struggle for his own interests, capable of the principle of sacrifice upon which the social integration rests, save only the Cause which expresses itself through the emotion of the ideal. Civilization has its origin, has its existence, and has the cause of its progress in the emotion of the ideal. It is through this faculty that the human mind rises to the Universal. It is his capacity for the emotion of the ideal and not his reasoning mind which constitutes Man the God-like, and which separates him from the brutes.

The first remarkable feature of the emotion of the ideal is that it is an attitude of mind which, for the deep physiological reasons to be referred to later, is most highly developed in the child. To produce the most permanent results—results which in most cases are ineradicable afterwards—the emotion of the ideal must always be appealed to in the mind of the child. One of the most significant passages in Mr. Bateson's essay dealing with inborn heredity in relation to society is that in which he recognizes, while not discussing the full bearing of the fact, that the altruistic emotions—which, as here stated, give that capacity for sacrifice upon which civilization is founded—are most highly developed in the young. As the inborn heredity of the individual of our existing civilization develops, "the altruistic emotions," Mr. Bateson asserts, tend " to weaken after adolescence and to disappear as middle age supervenes." [1]

This is a true observation, in which is recorded a fact, the application of which is of the widest reach and import in the future of civilization. The extraordinary intensity of the emotion of the ideal in the mind of the child, and the part which this faculty plays in producing that capacity for sacrifice upon which civilization rests, must always be kept in view. It is the basal fact in the science of cultural heredity. Mr. Havelock Ellis repeats Professor Stanley Hall's saying that " the normal child feels the heroism of the unaccountable instinct of self-sacrifice " at a very early age, even " far earlier and more keenly than it can understand the sublimity of truth." [2]   The bearing of this fact and its physiological import have only just begun to attract the attention of science.   But knowledge of it has for long governed the direction of development in the

[1] *Biological Fact and the Structure of Society.*
[2] *Man and Woman.*

higher movements in art, in religion, and in all great literatures.

The effect of the conceptions of mind conveyed to the young by training and example under the influence of the emotion of the ideal is absolutely ineradicable. It gives a permanent direction to character which can never be altered. It creates in the individual a capacity for sacrifice in the service of those ideals which rises above self-interest and which is entirely independent of the reasoning faculty of the human mind. In recent times the control of this limitless power through the direction of the emotion of the ideal in the young has been seen directed in its most characteristic forms to national ends. It has given in this connexion the astonishing examples of sacrifice which have been witnessed in the great world war that began in 1914.

Throughout this war the capacity for sacrifice in men has been exhibited on an unparalleled scale under the sternest conditions. It has been seen continuously enabling great aggregates of men, amounting in total to millions, to meet resolutely almost certain death in massed formation in the service of Germany. It produced the same examples of sacrifice on a stupendous scale in the case of other countries engaged in the war. It gave civilization the example of millions of men enrolled by Great Britain and her peoples by voluntary enlistment going to meet death in the service of their cause with a cheerful and considered judgment on a scale which under such conditions is without any precedent in history. But in all these cases it would be found on inquiry that the strength of the devotion compelling to sacrifice for the ideals of nationality owed nothing to the inborn heredity of the individual, but had its spring and origin in the first instance in the collective heredity imposed on the rising generation under the influence of the emotion of the ideal powerfully awakened by teaching and example at some stage in the mind of childhood.

An indirect influence of the capacity for sacrifice thus created is to be witnessed far beyond that stage described by Bateson in which the altruistic emotions tend to weaken and disappear. A powerful effect is to be seen in its influence on general opinion. For however selfish the general outlook may become, men still, as William James has asserted, "tolerate no one who has no capacity whatever for heroic sacrifice. . . . No matter what a man's frailties otherwise may be, if he is willing to risk death in the service he has chosen, the fact consecrates him for ever." [1]

It has been already said that the work done by

[1] *The Varieties of Religious Experience*, Lecture XIV. p. 364.

9

Germany in the creation and by the imposition on the rising generation of the collective idealisms of her nationality is the greatest event in modern history. It is a record, it is true, of immense power misdirected to atavistic ends. But this fact does not take from its significance. The true application of the lesson which it contains has yet to come within the full vision of civilization. It is exactly the lesson which I prophesied in the Herbert Spencer Lecture to the University of Oxford in 1908 that modern Germany had to deliver to the world.[1] It has become a lesson which must now, as a matter of life and death, be applied by civilization as soon as it is apprehended. It is, for this reason, of vital importance to concentrate attention on the mechanism of the process as it is to be seen actually in being.

In that process in modern Germany by which the psychology of a whole people was changed in a generation the fundamental fact to be grasped is that the seat and centre of the vast experiment throughout the whole period of accomplishment was in the mind of the young. It was the German educational system which created the psychology which carried modern Germany into the world war of 1914 with all its far-reaching consequences. The

[1] *Individualism and After*, pp. 30-1.

giving of definite direction to the German educational system was, moreover, the work of but a few persons. It was in the main the achievement of but two persons—of Adalbert Falk, Prussian Minister of Education up to 1879, and of the Emperor William II. In most countries the leaders of great national movements are looked for amongst the intellects that have been prominent in the various national activities and in the national systems of culture. But in Germany in this work it was different. In Prussia it was to the teachers of the elementary schools that the State looked first for support in its attempt to create the idealisms of German nationalism and to impose them on the young. After these it looked to the teachers of the higher schools and then to the university professoriate. It was only in the last phase that the adult mind of the nation was considered.

Soon after his accession the Emperor William II personally addressed the elementary and upper school teachers of his realms and laid before them his ideas as to the necessity of concentrating the mind of the young on national ideals through the scheme of education which was immediately afterwards imposed on the nation. In the address and in the scheme the idealization of war, the idealization of the German nation as resting on war, and the idealization of the part played in each by the House of Hohenzollern occupied a prominent place. The spirit of this speech and of the measures which followed it was carried afterwards into every detail of education by the whole organized power of the State in Germany.

The effect on the rising generation in Germany of this *auswärtige Kulturpolitik*, which may be translated to mean in practice the continuous presentation of national conceptions to the young mind of Germany under the influence of the emotion of the ideal, was profound. It is necessary to try to imagine, however imperfectly, what actually took place. The ideals which were set up were continuously impressed by teachers on the mind of the young of a whole people from the earliest age. We must get rid of the common and superficial notion that these ideals of German nationality could be visible to outsiders of other nations as they were visible to the German people. For the power of the whole experiment lay in this. The German system touched the springs of mind at its deepest psychological centres in always presenting the national aims closely associated with that conception of sacrifice and duty to which the emotion of the ideal is inseparably allied in the mind of the young.

The leading ideas underlying the German educational system bore in nearly all their features a strong resemblance to those propounded earlier by Mazzini to his countrymen.[1] Mazzini's clarion cry of the *ideal* re-echoes throughout it. The bearing, moreover, of Mazzini's profound distinction that *education* is addressed through emotion to the moral faculties in the young and *instruction* to the intellectual and that the life of a nation is always in its education was everywhere apprehended by the German mind.

It is necessary then to imagine this organized teaching of the ideal of German nationalism imposed on the young of the nation in the elementary schools following the youth of the country into the higher schools. It is necessary to consider it again following the rising generation into the universities at a more advanced stage. And still later it is necessary to imagine the whole adult nation with the same ideals preached to it continuously by officials, by the organized State, and last of all by the Emperor at the head of the State.

The higher collective policy of the State in the final stage was well described in a letter written in June 1913, a year before the outbreak of the great war, by Herr von Bethmann-Hollweg to Professor

[1] *On the Duties of Man*, IX. " Education."

Lamprecht of the University of Leipzig,[1] urging the constant support and co-operation of the educated classes in the work of keeping the national ideals before the German people. It was particularly defined with surprising earnestness, simplicity, and power by the Emperor William II in a long series of addresses, numbering nearly one thousand, during the first twenty-five years of his reign, delivered on occasions of nearly every type of public duty.

The aim of the State throughout this work was everywhere to orientate public opinion through the heads of both its spiritual and temporal departments, through the bureaucracy, through the officers of the army, through the State direction of the Press, and last of all through the State direction of the entire trade and industry of the nation, so as to bring the idealism of the whole people to a conception of and to a support of the national policy of modern Germany.

It is the emotion of the ideal that we have in view through all this stupendous making of history in modern Germany as it has influenced the world. It was the conception of duty and the capacity for sacrifice evoked in the mind of the young at an early stage through the emotion of the ideal on which

[1] " German Ideals," *Times*, 13 December 1913.

the whole fabric was based and in which the vitality of the whole conception lay.

This fact already remarked on as regards the schools is particularly in evidence in the Emperor's speeches on almost all matters.   In the Emperor's addresses to the recruits of the army and navy on the occasions of the annual swearings in and in his addresses to the army there was mingled even with that note of appeal to the primal instinct in man which on one occasion [1] drew severe condemnation from Tolstoy, the continuous note of the necessity for sacrifice, duty, discipline, devotion, iron obedience in the service of the national ideals.   On wider public occasions side by side with the extraordinary mixture of the ethics of Nietzsche and Haeckel with the ethics of Christianity it was still the inculcation of the spirit of the effort and the sacrifice needful in the service of the national ideals which constituted the most characteristic note in the Emperor's addresses—" To us, the German people, great ideals are a lasting possession . . . the fostering of the ideal is the greatest work of Culture." [2]

It is impossible to overestimate the influence of the emotion of the ideal in such a case.   It is the effect of the capacity for sacrifice which it produced

[1] The Emperor's Speech, Potsdam, 23 November 1891, on swearing in recruits.

[2] Speech, Berlin, 18 December 1901.

that resounds through the history of modern Germany. Even as applied therein to the realization of the lowest and coarsest aims of war the effect in organized form is such as to support fully the description used by the American writer already quoted of " almost superhuman." If the national ideals which were placed in the foreground had not been atavistic and had been in line with the meaning of evolving civilization it is not too much to say that there is nothing which modern Germany could not have accomplished in the world by the means that were employed.

The conclusion upon which the mind must be concentrated is that it is inevitable that civilization will look in future to the emotion of the ideal employed under such conditions for the accomplishment of its aims. The science of the function of the emotion of the ideal in the social integration that is proceeding is nothing more and is nothing less than the science of efficiency and therefore the science of all winning causes in civilization. The immeasurable futility of any other kind of knowledge appealing to us as the science of efficiency in civilization will gradually be borne in with conviction on the mind of the world. Once we have grasped the elemental difference between the cause of efficiency in the individual integration resting on self-assertion and the cause of efficiency in the social integration resting on selflessness, the fundamental importance of the emotion of the ideal as a cause of human progress becomes steadily visible.

It is the principles of the child mind in their relation to the capacity for sacrifice in the individual which underlie the ascending curve of efficiency in every social institution of the race. It is the mind of the child, before the child passes under the influence of that inborn heredity of the individual, efficient in the struggle for the possession of property, as described with such extraordinary illumination by Bateson, which constitutes the basal fact upon which the social integration is being reared.

Every organized force in civilization, from that of political parties and of the national life of peoples down to those represented by the vast hidden under-world of finance which wraps and enfolds all things, is grasping this fact by the fundamental instinct of its life—that the emotion of the ideal has become the first cause in the world to be reckoned with under modern conditions.

It was the emotion of the ideal, similarly applied through the collective inheritance imposed by the nation on the rising generation, and applied so as to bring into existence the strong sense of duty and

the capacity for sacrifice with which it is always
intimately allied in the minds of the young, which
created that other utterly unforeseen and incalculable phenomenon of the modern world, namely,
the new-born power·of Japan. There is still no
Western nation outside of Germany which has so
clearly apprehended the significance in the future
of the fact that the science of the emotion of the
ideal is the science of power in civilization. In all
her recent dealings with China it may be noticed
that behind the more sensational events that
excite the attention of politicians, it is the struggle
of Japan for the mind of the young and for control
of the schools, through which the young of the rising
generation can be influenced under the conditions
desired, which occupies consistently the attention of
the leaders of the Japanese nation.

That the result to be obtained in civilization by
the method of influencing the world through the
social inheritance as here described reduces to insignificance those possible by any eugenic scheme
whatsoever founded on the inborn heredity of the
individual, is a conclusion which comes to the mind
with great strength of conviction. The prolonged
concentration in the past of the intellect of the West
on the comparatively unimportant part played by
the inborn heredity of the individual in human

evolution, instead of on the immense function of the cultural heredity of society imposed on the mind of the young of each generation under the influence of the emotion of the ideal, is one of the most remarkable, as it is one of the most pregnant, facts in the history of mankind. It is a cause which has undoubtedly for long retarded the delayed development of civilization.

This fact is all the more striking, as there has been for a long period foreshadowed in the West in nearly every leading branch of the activities of the Western mind an instinctive perception of the true line which human evolution is taking, and of the importance in the development in civilization of qualities reaching their highest expression only in the mind of the young.

For instance, in science the fact has been on record that the development of the human face after childhood into the usual adult maturity, corresponding to the period wherein Bateson described the altruistic emotions as tending to weaken, represents development towards a type of face which for some unexplained cause is instinctively recognized by the mind as nearer the apelike in character.

Havelock Ellis, remarking on this fact, speaks of the type of face which the child represents as appearing to be for some reason the standard to which universal civilization is moving.[1]   In this connexion it has often been remarked, as we shall see in detail later, that the type of face amongst peoples of advanced civilization is quite distinctive in its youthfulness. Progress from savagery to civilization is marked by an increasing youthfulness of appearance amongst typical races in the advance upwards. Professor Chamberlain in his studies of the child mind has laid emphasis on a conclusion bearing in the same direction. The human child, he considers, acquires a more apelike appearance as it advances towards the adult stage. When the individual enters upon that mature stage after adolescence discussed by Mr. Bateson, in which it is stated that the altruistic feelings begin to fail and disappear, there has been lost in him what Professor Chamberlain calls " the comparative ultra-human characteristics of his early childhood." The qualities foreshadowed in the child, he adds in another chapter, " seem to be those which will one day be the most valued possession of the race." [2]

Again it may be noticed that the instinct that the qualities which reach their highest development in the young are related to the highest standards of

[1] *Man and Woman.*

[2] A. F. Chamberlain, *The Child : a Study in the Evolution of Man.*

civilization in the future, is expressed with remarkable strength and consistency throughout all the
higher phases of Western Art.   Every student
who has reached the last meanings of Greek Art
will have come in view sooner or later of the fact
that there was a clear conception of the Greek mind
ever seeking with great force to express itself
through Greek Art.   He will have come to the conviction that it was in its representations of the
quality of the childlike in the human face that
Greek Art struggled to express its highest content.
In this effort of the Greek genius to reproduce the
content of the child mind in its representations of
the human face, the beholder, in short, is witnessing
nothing less than the sustained attempt of this
surprisingly endowed Western people thus to utter
the soul of the world through the medium of its
art.

It is the note of this struggle which re-echoes
throughout all Western art down to the present
time.   The instinctive perception of the superiority
and of the supremacy of the child mind in civilization is witnessed in all the higher phases of Western
literature.   The conception that genius represents
or is closely allied to the childlike and that the
mark of both is their superior relationship to the
universal permeates all the literature of the West,

as indeed it does to a lesser degree all the great literatures of the world. It is a similar note which characterizes the inner life of all the higher forms of religion. " Except ye become as little children " ye cannot enter the higher life or see with the higher vision is the sustained expression of this fact in the Christian religion.

The evolutionary bearing of these phenomena cannot be mistaken. Once there has been grasped the central significance of the emotion of the ideal in relation to collective efficiency and of the circumstance that it is only in the mind of the child that the emotion of the ideal can be evoked in the conditions in which it produces its highest, its most permanent, and its most transforming results upon the cultural heredity of civilization, the reach of the facts is evident. A knowledge of the meaning of such facts is the first step to the science of power in civilization. For what we are really watching in the phenomena described is the gradual emergence into view of what has become the principal cause of collective efficiency in the era of the social integration of the world.

The overmastering and revolutionary effect of the emotion of the ideal in the mind of the child directed through the cultural inheritance of civilization cannot be better exemplified than by attempting to imagine it in operation in the most difficult and extreme example which it is possible to conceive.

The most distant ideal, in the sense of being the most remote from realization, which the human mind could possibly have set before itself in the West for some generations past has been the ideal of permanent universal peace. The utter remoteness of the prospect under existing conditions was visible to all thinking minds immediately before the outbreak of the world war in 1914. It was visible in the spectacle of the armed and arming nations of civilization getting down to the first principles of force. But it was apparent also for a deeper reason through another fact, namely, the nature of the case for peace which had come to be presented by pacifists to the world.

In the case for peace, as it had come to be put before the war which began in 1914, peace was urged upon civilization, not because it was an object worthy of the vastest sacrifice in its attainment, but because it was the sound economic policy of the nations. War was condemned vehemently, not because it was the last crime of civilization, but because it was held to be a great illusion to believe that it was a more profitable national policy than peace.   It would of course be quite unfair to imagine this as the full meaning of the case for peace, for the spirit if not the form of the propaganda rose far above this level in most minds.   Yet the fact remained that war was denounced essentially not as war but as the policy which, to use Sir William Robertson Nicoll's scathing phrase, " would postpone the blessed hour of tranquil money getting." [1]

The inherent hopelessness of attempting to convert a warring world to a policy of universal peace with such a creed stood revealed to all thinking minds.   For the first credential of every living movement in civilization is the capacity for sacrifice which it is able to create, sacrifice at whatever cost for the ends believed in.   Even the creed of war demanding as it has continuously done the greatest sacrifice of which human nature is capable for its cause, was immeasurably nobler and greater than the creed of peace as thus declared.

Now it is evident that no doctrine of interests can ever abolish war.   In civilization where the first principle of life is sacrifice any utilitarian creed of conduct whatsoever founded on the greatest material interest of the existing individual is always and essentially what Mr. Arthur Balfour once luminously defined systems of opinion of this type

[1] *British Weekly*, 3 June 1915.

to be—*parasitic*. It may flourish in the midst of the other life around it, but it has no roots of its own and it will wilt in the first stress of realism. Nothing can supersede war in civilization except some cause strong enough to overwhelm and control that inborn heredity of the fight in man which has come down in him from all the ages of the past and which has been carried by him in particular into every institution of Western civilization.

Can such a cause ever exist in the world ? To imagine it universally operative between nations there is no answer but to turn to a cause now operative between men within the civil law of civilization.

To the average man it scarcely ever occurs to imagine the reason why the ordinary law-abiding, honour-respecting citizen whom he meets in daily life observes the law of civilization and never dreams of becoming a swindler or a highwayman. To the mind which is simply shrewd the overruling reason seems to be that in civilization a well-organized system of society resting on law, which rests in turn on irresistible force, makes such a course unreasonable by rendering it a venture foolish and unprofitable in the extreme for any person to attempt to break the law. That honesty is the best policy just as peace is urged as the best policy is regarded as a quite obvious and sufficient reason for pursuing it.

Yet how utterly wide of the truth such an answer would be. The ordinary law-abiding citizen does not break the law and does not become a swindler or a highwayman. But not for any cause which rests on any reasoning of this kind. He does not break the law simply because it is impossible for him to do so. It would be impossible for him to do so if there were no self-interest of this nature to warn him, and no irresistible force to overtake him, and no organized system of society to punish him. He cannot break the law, not because he fears civil punishment, but because he knows beyond doubt that however successfully he might hope to attempt it, however great the gain which he might expect to secure from it—it would be of no use to him. For he would have lost by the act all that makes life worth living in losing the internal standard of himself which he carries in his mind.

At some stage of his career, in short, the average individual of civilization whom we meet on every side of us has passed permanently under the influence of the emotion of the ideal. It was conveyed to him by teaching or example through the cultural inheritance. And he has, thereby, passed irre-

vocably into another world. He can never free
himself from the influence of that internal standard
which has been set up within him. It will pursue
him to the end. Thompson invoked it as the Hound
of Heaven. "I fled him," he groaned in his
anguish, "down the nights and down the days, I
fled him down the arches of the years, I fled him
down the labyrinthine ways of my own mind."
But in vain! Never can the individual escape
the pursuer, never can he revert to be the man
he would otherwise have become. Even the
lowest and meanest individual is in such circumstances capable of the most surprising degree of
sacrifice before he will prove entirely unfaithful to
that unseen internal standard which he carries in
his inner mind.

This miracle takes place around us in the world
on a universal scale in every generation. There is
no way the human mind can conceive in which war
can be abolished amongst nations except by a
similar miracle. Universal peace can only be
secured in one way—by raising the mind of civilization, through the emotion of the ideal conveyed to
the rising generation by the collective inheritance,
to a plane where the barbarism of war would be
so abhorrent to it that the degradation of engaging
in it would take away from a people that principal

motive of self-respect which makes life worth living.

Given clear vision in the general mind, this cultural inheritance, utterly impossible as it might seem, could be imposed on civilization in a single generation. Only in a condition of the world in which such a collective inheritance would be imposed on the mind of each generation is it possible to conceive international law ever becoming endowed with the same irresistible authority among nations as the civil law now possesses amongst men. Only in such circumstances is it possible to conceive material force reduced to that legitimate function among nations which it now occupies in civil life, namely, the protection under the direction of civilization of the higher and more developed standards of the race against what would then become the criminal standards of the less-evolved societies of men.

It is evident on reflection that there is no goal to which the emotion of the ideal thus directed is not capable of carrying the human mind. Fitfully and ignorantly as it has been employed in the past, it is the cause which has been behind all the progress of the world. It is capable of accomplishing any purpose to which it may be steadily directed over long periods of time. It is the nature of the inner vision which it brings into being, that it leaves the possessor never satisfied with the world as it is, and that it drives him through every degree of effort to endeavour to realize his ideal. Evoked under suitable conditions in the mind of the young, it is able to render the successive generations of men upon whom it acts fixed of purpose, capable of the most surprising labours, and sufficient to otherwise impossible measures of self-subordination and self-sacrifice.

It is in this cause of the emotion of the ideal that we have undoubtedly the springs of all power in the modern conditions of the world. It is no exaggeration but a sober statement of fact to say that it is capable of sweeping out of civilization in a single generation any institution, or any order of society, or any inheritance of the past. Although it has never been organized in the science of civilization on a vast scale in modern conditions it has been the cause which every leader of men has employed in the past. Every deep-seeing mind of the race— from the founders of its first religions, from Plato in his groping after the meaning of the soul in the Phaedrus, from the prophets of Hebraism and the leaders of Christianity down to the seers of the current age—has felt the illimitable significance of the emotion of the ideal in the development of the world. It is the characteristic cause of the social integration, the cause which Mr. Compton Leith attempted to define to us in *Sirenica* when he described it as a passion more powerful in man than any animal desire.

The science of this Cause is the science of power in civilization. The manner in which it constructively works in the individual mind is well described by James in his *Text Book of Psychology*, although he did not touch those wider collective aspects to be discussed later in Chapter IX.[1] A leader-writer in the *Times*[2] recently accurately described the emotion of the ideal, when he spoke of it as giving that inward call in the human mind under the influence of which every human institution has the power of prophesying to us its finer self so as to make us for ever discontented with its present state.

Under this influence the human mind rises permanently above all reasoned theories of utilitarian conduct. It is thus that the higher religious beliefs of the world have permanently influenced successive generations of men to seek to reach those apparently unattainable inward ideals of perfection which it is characteristic of every living religion that it sets before its adherents. It is thus that Professor Gilbert Murray saw the Greek mind in

[1] See p. 227.   [2] *Times*, 25 October 1913.

the development of the Greek epic endeavouring to cast off in history the brute inheritance of the past of the race.[1]   It is thus we behold the passion of the Absolute in the soul of the poet and the artist challenging the world for an ideal which has never yet been realized.

Every mind of the race possessing the vision of genius has at some moment felt thus the illimitable superiority of the emotion of the ideal to every other human quality.   " It is not by anything written since the beginning in textbooks of social science that the world has advanced," said Mr. H. G. Wells on one occasion to the writer.   " The human mind has always accomplished progress by its construction of Utopias."   This is a true saying. It has been the emotion of the ideal which has brought to the harvest of action the souls of all the leaders of all the causes which have been since the world began.   How to organize this illimitable Cause under the conditions of the modern world is the problem before the human spirit.   The master fact of the social integration is that the science of power in civilization is the science of the passion for the ideal.   The passion for the ideal is the passion of perfection, which is the passion for God.

[1] *Rise of the Greek Epic.*

CHAPTER VI

THE STUPENDOUS POSITION IN
THE WEST

IN the vast problems with which the Western mind is struggling in history there are thus, it will be seen, two distinct but absolutely opposing sides. For centuries past the attention of the Western intellect has been concentrated on the forces on one side only of this problem. From time immemorial the dominant theme of the West has been everywhere the same—the activities of the individual successful in the struggle for his own interests. It is the science of these activities, the heredity of this individual, the laws of this struggle, which constitute the principal sum of Western knowledge and which have contributed the main elements of Western history. The era of evolution which this development represents is the era of the integration of the individual. And Darwin, and Darwin only, is the true exponent of the natural laws of the phase in human history in which it culminates.

On the other side of the picture there is now the surprising opposing phenomenon in the West of the gathering of the forces which represent the supersession or the negation of every one of the ruling principles of this era of the past.   For the goal towards which the face of civilization is set is not the individual integration but the social integration.   It is in the social integration that the soul of the world is being brought to the birth.   And the laws of the social integration are not the laws of the individual integration.   It is not in the heredity inborn in civilized man, so accurately described by Bateson, but in the immeasurably more important cultural heredity imposed on civilized man by civilization itself through the action of the emotion of the ideal on the young of each generation that we have the cause of efficiency and the seat of power in the future of the world.

This is the basal fact which underlies all phases of the life of the West.   The powerful and universal interests of civilization are already instinctively conscious of it.   They may be observed on every side staging themselves, often with the strangest Caliban-like' movements, into the particular attitudes which represent this knowledge.   Throughout the West all institutions in which power is centred, from the military empires to international organizations of finance, feel themselves to be envisaged with conditions wherein the past has ceased to be a guide to them. Absorbed in the seething struggle of the time they know by a sure instinct of their life that the emotion of the ideal in the general mind is a cause of the first magnitude to be reckoned with in the future. But the fact which has to be noticed, standing out above other phenomena, is that the interests which have hitherto ruled in the West do not understand the function of the emotion of the ideal, and are proving themselves unable to reckon with it. They are like organisms in an environment to which they have no developed organs of correspondence.

In the marshalling of forces in the present conditions of the West it may be observed that the stake for which nearly all the desperately in earnest combatants are playing in the last resort is to win to their side and to organize in their interests the emotion of the ideal in the general mind. Yet there is nothing within the range of human experience to compare with the actual fact of the failure throughout the West to employ in the cause of civilization the emotion of the ideal in any of its forms. The American writer already quoted regarded the attempt made to direct the mind of the German people for two generations to support the ideals which resulted in the world war of 1914 as one of the most pathetic instances in the history of mankind of colossal power misconceived and misdirected. But the full truth goes much further than this. The Western mind has, in reality, almost completely missed in every form the employment in the service of civilization of the emotion of the ideal. And where it has hitherto sought to employ this illimitable cause it has hitherto only directed it to some aim so essentially barbarous and monstrous in conception that the effort has been fore-doomed from the outset to failure.

What is the explanation of this strange and stupendous position in the West ? The emotion of the ideal when directed by civilization is a cause so potent to transform the world that there is practically nothing which cannot be achieved through it, even, as we have seen, to the complete altering of the psychology of a people in a single generation. It is the cause in the function of which the whole social integration centres. Why then has the mind of the West so completely missed or misconceived this function ? Why should a cultured mind of the East strike a note which rings true in describing Western science as no more than ignorant knowledge ? Why after centuries of industrial progress should we have still throughout

the West the economic system, untouched by the
slightest breath of collective idealism, against which
Marx declared the social war or against which
a President of the United States formulated the
terrible indictment that it is only a struggle for
interests, of which the law is, " Let everyone look
out for himself : let every generation look out
for itself : while we reared giant machinery which
made it impossible for any but those who stood at
the levers of control to have a chance to look out
for themselves " ? [1]   Above all, why in the single
instance in which the West has hitherto grasped
the conception of employing the emotion of the
ideal on a large scale towards a collective aim,
namely, in organizing nations for war, has it hitherto
only directed it to results so atavistic and so devastating that for a thousand years Western civilization has rendered universal history synonymous
with universal homicide ?

Now if we regard the history of the West in the
past, the first fact which stands out before the
imagination is the overwhelming and dominating
influence of the heredity of the fight in all Western
peoples.   The peoples of the West represent, it
has been already said, the largest, the most intense,

<hr>

[1] " Inaugural Address of President Dr. Woodrow Wilson,
1913," *Times*, 5 March 1913.

and most prolonged process of military selection in the world. For thousands of years before the dawn of history the West has been the seat of the highest expression of force representing the highest expression of the individual efficient in the fight for his own interests. The consequences of this fact are felt to-day throughout every fibre of Western civilization. It is the qualities of the fight (the qualities, that is to say, dominant in the age of evolution when the universal effort of the efficient individual of the race was for A to endeavour to kill B before B was able to kill A) which survive in overwhelming strength in all Western institutions.

If we turn now and regard the collective attempts made in the history of the West to employ the emotion of the ideal collectively as a creative and transforming cause in relation to the cultural inheritance of civilization, the spectacle which is presented in these conditions has most remarkable features.

By far the greatest attempt hitherto made by the West to apply the emotion of the ideal to the cultural inheritance of civilization has been made through Christianity. In this religion the social passion transfigures and transcends all other emotions. The sanction for sacrifice is the greatest that can be conceived. Christianity was accepted by the West, and has been for centuries taught by the West throughout the world, as the religion of universal peace. It is essentially, among all religions, the religion of brotherhood, of love, of goodwill among men. It proclaims these conditions uncompromisingly as universal, as operative beyond the boundaries of all creeds, and as extending even to enemies. It recognizes neither race nor colour nor nationality in the presence of the all-subordinating ideals which it uplifts. The essence of these ideals, as it was recently described with great insight and accuracy in a leading article in the *Times*, is the fact of what was apparently the most complete and terrible of world failures becoming, because of that apparent failure and only through it, the most incredible triumph over all the powers of the world.[1]

Yet the result, if it could only be seen by a mind absolutely free from the prepossessions in which we are steeped, is one which would stagger the imagination. The terrible dominating heredity of the fight inborn in the West has made of this ideal throughout history a cause of blood and war and of world-embracing conflict. The unfolding of the Christian religion in the West has been a record of fighting and slaughter aiming at worldly triumph which is absolutely unparalleled in any other phase of the

[1] *Times*, 21 March 1913.

history of the race.   In all the developments in which we see the West endeavouring to present to the human mind the tremendous ideals of the Christian religion, one aim seems almost invariably at some stage to become dominant in the fighting mind of those who have held power in the West. In the development of its churches, of its creeds, of its nationalities, of its theories of the State in relation to civilization, the West has continuously made interpretations of the interest or of the aims of the Christian religion, or of some system of national policy proceeding from them, the occasion for entrenching itself in absolutisms always resting on force, always organized by force, and always aiming directly or indirectly to impose themselves by force on other people.

The principal theme of the history of the West is the theme of these universal wars of slaughter carried on by nations and peoples in the name of the principles of the religion of universal peace.   In these conflicts, despite all appearances to the contrary, right, truth, and justice have been almost without exception, just as in the pagan world, made to rest in the last resort on successful force.   The combatants on each side proclaim the principles of Christianity to be part of their cause.   And after their victories they carry the battle-stained banners

of their wars even into the churches and temples
of the Christian religion, exactly in the manner of
the pagan systems of old, in which truth and
right were no more than local expressions of successful force.   Western civilization throughout
history has professed to be the civilization founded
on Christianity.   Yet almost every development of
the West has been based on war, and has taken
place with the menace of war or the fact of war
accompanying and pervading it.

The terrible individual heredity of the fighting
male of the West is so blinding to the mind in all its
effects that the violent contradictions of standards
which it provokes mostly pass absolutely unnoticed.
Men of culture, and even the actual leaders and
teachers of Christianity, seem quite unconscious of
the spirit of a contradiction which in actual fact exceeds anything that has been witnessed in the world
under any other standards. The spectacle of the West,
for more than a thousand years under the influence
of the inborn heredity of the fight in its ruling
classes, devastating the world with war in the name
of the religion of universal peace, will beyond doubt
strike the mind of the world in the future as probably the most monstrous phenomenon in the
history of humanity.

The spirit of the fight which accompanies and

produces this contradiction pervades all phases of Western life, political and economic alike. It has sterilized for centuries every attempt to apply the emotion of the ideal in the service of civilization. Any detached mind which takes its way through the notable charters, speeches, bulls, greater State documents, and social pronouncements in which the vital decisions of the West have been put on record, will receive this conviction with overwhelming strength. The influence, moreover, of the blighting cause which has prevented the West from utilizing the function of the emotion of the ideal in the service of civilization has never been more powerful and more all-pervading than in the time in which we are living.

For two generations past the dominant feature of the history of the West has been nothing else than the struggle of the comparatively small class who have held military power in modern Germany against the soul of the world. History has produced no more striking set of documents than those in which the phases of this gigantic conflict are recorded. And there are no more characteristic documents in this collection than the public utterances made during his reign of the Emperor William II. It would be impossible to have in evidence in more impressive form than in these addresses the clash of the stand-

II

ards of two epochs of time as it existed in the mind
of the sovereign who more than any single individual
held military power concentrated in his hand, and
who at the same time grasped even in the midst of
the struggle the overwhelming collective significance
of the emotion of the ideal in the future of the
world.

For instance, we witness this Western ruler on his
accession to the throne in 1888 addressing his people
as a Christian sovereign,[1] extolling the acts " born
of Christian humility," and vowing to God " to be
a righteous and gentle Prince." We turn back a
few pages, and then behold him almost simultaneously addressing the army. The reader seems to
live in another world. Instantly the army is placed
before the nation. The heredity of another epoch
of time seems to dominate every thought and utterance. In the address to the army we behold force
as the ultimate fact of the world. It is the depend-
ence of the Emperor's ancestors on the army which
is emphasized as the vital and significant fact in the
history of the State. " So we are bound together,"
the address continues, " I and the army—so are we

---

[1] In this and the references to the Emperor's speeches which
immediately follow, the text quoted is that in the translation of
Christian Gauss, Professor of Modern Languages, Princeton
University, who has dealt only with the speeches which he
states to have received official or semi-official sanction.

born for one another . . . you are now about to
swear to me the oath of fidelity and obedience, and
I vow that I shall ever be mindful of the fact that
the eyes of my forefathers look down upon me from
that other world, and that I one day shall have to
render up to them an account of the fame and the
honour of the army." [1]

In the spirit of this extraordinary document the
atmosphere of the modern West falls away from us
as if it had never existed.   The reader would experience no surprise if, unconscious of its historical
associations, he were informed that it was the record
of a speech of some ruler of men to his army made
anywhere on this planet ten thousand years ago.

This conflict of standards in which the Western
heredity of the fight in the individual struggles with
and at times completely dominates the spirit of the
Christian religion is visible continuously in almost
every page of this notable record.   Again and again
in the Emperor's addresses throughout his reign
the spirit of the Christian religion appears to be
uppermost.   The standards of Christianity are held
high before the German nation as ideals.   His
soldiers, he tells them, as in the address on ad-
ministering the oath to recruits in Berlin in 1897,
must be good Christians.   But ever and again it

[1] *Op. cit.*   [2] *Op. cit.*

is as if we were ushered suddenly into another world. In the address at Potsdam in 1891, when the feeling against socialists ran high, these same Christian soldiers were told that " more and more unbelief and discontent raise their heads in the Fatherland, and it may come to pass that you will have to shoot down or stab your own relatives and brothers. Then seal your loyalty with your heart's blood ! " [1] This was the pronouncement which roused Tolstoy to describe as an " abyss of degradation " the condition which the recruits reached when they promised obedience. And he called the world to witness the paralysing self-contradiction and self-stultification of the West, when " men —Christians, liberals, cultured men of our time, all of them—are not only not provoked by this insult, but do not even notice it." [2]

The heredity of the fight allied to uncontrolled power in the mind of the West is capable of producing results so extreme that without the facts in evidence they could scarcely have been conceived. In his address at Bremen in March 1905 on the mission of Germany, the Emperor put aside on behalf of the German nation all dreams of empty world empire. " I have made a vow," he continued, " never to strive for an empty world dominion.

[1] *Op. cit.*   [2] *Op. cit.*

For what has become of the so-called world empires ? Alexander the Great, Napoleon I—all the great warriors — have swum in blood. . . . The world empire of which I have dreamed shall consist in this, that a newly-created German empire shall first of all enjoy on all sides the most absolute confidence as a quiet, honourable, and peaceful neighbour ; and that . . . it shall not be founded upon acquisitions won with the sword, but upon the mutual trust of the nations who are striving for the same goal." [1]

This pronouncement in which we seem to see the spirit of Christianity uppermost must be kept in view to gauge to the full the extent of the position of self-stultification in which the West is locked.   For it proceeded, it must be remembered, from the absolute ruler of the nation which was compelled by its ruling classes to play Germany's part immediately after in the world war of 1914, with all its consequences to neighbouring States and to the whole world ; the State whose diplomacy and policy was being almost at the same time defined by its military writers like Von Bernhardi as resting not on " the most absolute confidence on all sides," but, as it was frankly expressed in Bernhardi's words, " simply and solely on power and expediency."   It was the utterance,

[1] *Op. cit.*

moreover, of the supreme military head of the nation, whose General Military Staff issued soon after for the instruction of German officers the *Kriegsbrauch im Landkriege*, in which every ethic of the German State at war is made to turn similarly to power and expediency applied in the most terrible conditions of war.

For to quote again Professor J. H. Morgan's summary of some of the *Kriegsbrauch im Landkriege* rules of war: "Should they (the peaceful inhabitants of an invaded country) be exposed to the fire of their own troops? Yes: it may be indefensible, but its main justification is that it is successful. Should prisoners of war be put to death? It is always ugly, but it is sometimes expedient. May one hire an assassin, or corrupt a citizen, or incite an incendiary? Certainly: it may not be reputable and honour may fight shy of it, but the law of war is less touchy. Should the women and children, the old and the feeble, be allowed to depart before a bombardment begins? On the contrary, their presence is greatly to be desired; it makes the bombardment all the more effective."[1]

In all this picture of the illimitable genius of humanity directed thus to monstrous ends, a feature upon which special attention has to be fixed is the

[1] *Vide* p. 71.

effect of the concentration of power in a few hands. The fact has great significance in the future of democracy.   For it is in such conditions of power, even where they prevail in institutions outwardly representative in character, that the primitive inborn heredity of the fight in the individual struggles with and, in the end, completely dominates the cultural heredity which is imposed on the individual by civilization.

After Christianity, nationality has been the principal institution through which the West has sought to apply the emotion of the ideal on a collective scale in the service of civilization.   But the inborn heredity of the fight in vast strength has everywhere throughout the West carried the expressions of nationality into similar forms of combativeness.

In the result we see nearly every function of nationality amongst Western peoples diverted, just as in the pagan world, to some expression of exclusiveness, with the ultimate fact of war in the background. The appeal to the emotion of the ideal through nationality in the West has, in short, ever been an appeal to the instinct of combativeness, and nearly always with the conception of war in the background. Every living nation idealizes itself. But throughout the West the idealization

of a people through nationality has almost invariably taken the form of idealization in contrast to,
or in opposition to, some other people or nation.
Western history displays an ascending curve of
slaughter as it rises to the Armageddon of 1914
which furnishes an example of the instinct of
combativeness expressing itself through nationality
that would be absolutely incredible if we were not
familiarized with it and if we had received it as the
record of some savage order of the world.

Even within national frontiers the influence of
this heredity of the fight pervades all forms of the
national consciousness of the Western races. When
we see a leader like Mazzini dreaming of the high
ideals of the Italian nation in its relations to the
wider fellowship of humanity, we behold him driven
by necessity inherent in his environment still
thinking and reasoning in terms of combativeness
and force.

" What we have to do to establish the new order,"
he tells his fellow-countrymen, " is to overthrow by
force the brute force which opposes itself to-day to
every attempt at improvement." [1]   And what we
see Mazzini thinking in Italy in the first half of the
nineteenth century is precisely what the *Westminster Gazette* sees the leaders of democracy thinking

[1] *On the Duties of Man,* I. " To the Italian Working Man."

nearly a century later in England when it deplores the fact that the internal politics of the British nation are becoming " battles rather than delibera-tions, and that it has become in our time" the practice of all minorities "to threaten to carry on every controversy by violent and extra constitutional means even when Parliament has decided against them."

Nor is there any essential change in the note of all-pervading combativeness when the horizon of that class - consciousness which expresses itself externally and internally in nationalism extends into organizations world-wide in their aims. The principal opponents in Germany against whom the extreme sentiments of the speech of the Emperor William II at Potsdam, already quoted, were sup-posed to be directed, were the socialists who followed Karl Marx.   But we have only to read with insight to see that in the pages of Marx's *Kapital,* as in the Emperor's addresses, the distinctive fact is that we are in the presence of the same furious heredity of the fight.   It is only the conditions which have changed.   In Marx the national war has become the social war, and the frontiers of Marx's Fatherland have become extended to those of international socialism.   But we are still only in the presence of the primitive Darwinian man whose heredity

Bateson so accurately described to us as furnishing only one universal motive of action, namely, that which drives him in the struggle with somebody else for the possession of property.

And when we turn from Marx's programme of socialism in the pages of *Kapital* to Professor Karl Pearson's programme of socialism in the *Ethic of Free Thought*, it continues still to be the same spirit. Professor Pearson draws in academic seclusion in England the picture of his new order of society under socialism. And then the frantic heredity of the fighting male of the West takes possession of his soul. To those who offend against the laws of public property in Professor Pearson's new order of society it is to be, to use his actual words before quoted, " short shrift and the nearest lamp-post." The rules of the *Kriegsbrauch im Landkriege* could hardly furnish a more characteristic example of the spirit of the Darwinian man. The self-stultification of the West is, in short, as complete and as absolute at the hands of the socialistic Professor in England as Tolstoy considered it to be at the hands of the Christian Emperor in Germany. And the tragic irony of it is that, in this case also, Tolstoy would have had equal cause for saying that persons of culture, liberals, even the fellow-men of free thought whom Professor Pearson is addressing, are "not only not provoked by the insult, but do not even notice it."

The history of the emotion of the ideal in the West, in short, has been the same in all its principal manifestations. When controlled by those who have held power, especially when power has been concentrated in few hands, it has ever tended to be directed and dominated by the qualities of the primitive heredity of the fight. In the propagandas of parties and the marshalling and organizing of the great forces of the day, the orientation of all the arguments, of all the interests, is instinctively, as just observed, towards the emotion of the ideal in the general mind. But the failure of this effort in every form is one of the most marked features of the time. It is a fact that the mind of the West, on the whole, has completely failed to understand the emotion of the ideal. It has not grasped either the nature, or the magnitude, or the management of its function in the future of civilization. The only medium through which it has hitherto attempted to utilize collectively this transforming cause of the future in imposing the cultural inheritance of civilization on the general mind, on a universal scale, has been through the primitive and characteristic instinct of combativeness.

The level at which the argument proceeds in any great question of the day in the West is, therefore, above everything remarkable. It is almost as if we saw continuously the leaders of civilized men making an appeal before an audience of savages. It is the same kind of emotions which are being stirred, the same feelings of combativeness which are being aroused, the same kind of arguments which are being used. Every device, every ruse, every absurdity, even to grotesque distortions of the truth, are pressed into service to move or excite the feelings of combativeness.

It is a wonderful sight. As party government has developed in the West under democratic institutions, a new world of literature and art has come into existence in the press to supply all the machinery of this appeal to the instinct of combativeness. Every capable editor understands that in all the leading questions of the day the most effective appeal to the multitude is the emotional appeal through the spirit of combativeness. An appeal to the pure instinct of the fight or to that class consciousness upon which combativeness is based, and which man shares with the animal world, is known to be the most direct and effective means of moving the general mind on public questions.

In such circumstances, the standards of effective-

ness which have come to prevail in the press of
Western countries in the midst of the struggle of
commercial and financial interests on the one side
and the war of political parties on the other, are
altogether remarkable.   Until recently in the West
the press had been, after the organized institutions
of Christianity, the greatest agent in moving the
world through the emotion of the ideal.   Its
activities have been one of the main ultimate facts
upon which Western liberties have rested.   Its
spokesmen have exercised in the past an influence
exceeding a thousandfold that of the orators of the
Pnyx in ancient Athens in creating and sustaining
in the imagination of the multitude the ideas
through which the cultural inheritance of civilization was imposed on the people.   But the conditions of the past have been profoundly altered
as the press has passed, like all other institutions, under the sway of the dominant forces of the
time.

Mr. R. Donald, the editor of the London *Daily
Chronicle*, speaking recently in Great Britain as
President of the Institute of Journalists, described
in a remarkable address [1] the great revolution
which the British press has undergone in this respect
in less than a generation.   The leading feature of

[1] *Times*, 19 August 1913.

the change, as stated by Mr. Donald, is that the press had been commercialized on a gigantic scale. The central fact of this transition is that corporate ownership of the joint-stock type is superseding individual ownership of the idealist type. The effect of this, coupled with other changes, was, he said, to " place enormous power to sway public opinion in the hands of a few people." It was an inherent feature of these agglomerations, he continued, that they were controlled by exactly the same forces which operated in other fields of financial and commercial activity. Under the old system the proprietor " preferred less profit to compromise with principle," but under the new the culminating aim is necessarily the payment of dividends. "Dividends," said Mr. Donald, "must be earned even if principle is to suffer in the process."

The conditions under which the work of publicity is done in the midst of this raging war of interests, both external and internal, in which the press itself has become centrally engaged, have been described recently in striking and earnest language by more than one experienced observer. A writer in the *British Review* put in moderate language the party feature of it as seen from the outside in saying that the public is becoming uneasily aware that " a fair presentment of the truth is not the main object." [1] Mr. Chesterton, writing as an experienced journalist, has described the struggle as he saw it from the inside in the press itself. He sketched in a few bold and vivid strokes the work as it proceeded in the office of an effective newspaper. In the conditions which prevail, Mr. Chesterton saw the directing mind continually abolishing truth as Turner abolished a tower because it did not suit him. He described him, as it were, the arch creator of fact, with the great instrument of publicity in his hands, daily plunging a whole people into darkness, as Rembrandt would plunge a whole picture into darkness—to bring out a purpose. He saw him as the master artist of his time, at work upon events effacing and disguising the lineaments of affairs as Whistler would efface the lineaments of a woman —so that more important matters should not be interfered with. [2]

This description of the inside conditions of the press as they prevailed in one of the freest countries of the West in the first quarter of the twentieth century is of the profoundest interest. The calculated lightness of touch only adds to the significance as we read between the lines. It was written at a time when Great Britain was at peace with all the world, at a period when all the commercial and

---

[1] *British Review*, December 1913. [2] *Ibid.*

industrial interests of the West were in the full flush of the highest prosperity. It was given on first-hand knowledge by one of the foremost of British journalists. But as we scrutinize the description, the extraordinary import of it grips and even shocks the mind.

Two years later, most of the principal countries of the world had closed in the greatest war of all time. The public press in the greater part of the Western world was held, as it had never before been held in history, in the dominant grasp of an all-embracing military censorship. The surprising significance of the fact just referred to is this. Reading Mr. Chesterton's description now it seems to be, line for line and word for word, almost an exact description of the conditions of the press which prevailed in the principal countries of the West under the most ruthless form of military censorship to which public news and public opinion on a large scale has ever been subjected.

For during the Armageddon truth in the press throughout the greater part of Western civilization was indeed abolished—because it was not suitable. Peoples were, indeed, daily plunged into darkness on a universal scale—to bring out a purpose. The faces and lineaments of men and affairs were indeed effaced—so that they should not interfere with more important matters. Yet Mr. Chesterton's description was a description of the conditions prevailing in the press in one of the foremost countries in the world with regard to its social, political, and industrial affairs in a time of peace and under normal conditions. No more searching indictment of our civilization was ever written. It brings out the meaning of our Western life in these normal conditions as with a flash of universal illumination. It is a state of permanent war — relentless, remorseless, truth-extinguishing, primitive war throughout all our institutions, national and political, social and economic.

And the tragic irony of it in this case also is that Tolstoy would again have equal cause for saying that " men,—Christians, liberals, cultured men of our time, all of them "—can listen to these and similar descriptions of our current institutions and remain unconscious of their significance and of the self-stultification of our civilization which they imply. " They are not only not provoked by the insult ; they do not even notice it ! "

This is the condition to which the long intensive heredity of the fight inborn in the man of the West has carried civilization. It is the culminating phase of the epoch of the individual integration ; the epoch, that is to say, of the ascendancy in the world of the individual efficient in the struggle for his own interests.   The future lies in the social integration. The social integration rests on organization.   And in this organization the seat of efficiency and the centre of all power in the future is in that cultural heredity which civilization imposes on the individual through the emotion of the ideal.   There is practically nothing which cannot be accomplished through the emotion of the ideal in civilization.   There is absolutely no aim, which civilization chooses to set before itself, which it is not possible for civilization to achieve, even to the sweeping away of this existing world and the creation of a new world in a brief space of time.   The great question of the age, the question to which all others are subordinate is: Where are we to look in the new order for the psychic centre of this cultural heredity of civilization ?

PART III

THE NEW PSYCHIC CENTRE OF POWER

CHAPTER VII

FIRST LAWS OF THE SCIENCE OF POWER

WHEN the mind of the West comes to grasp in all its far-reaching applications the fact that the Science of Power in the social integration is the science of directing the collective will over long stretches of time to definite ends through the emotion of the ideal, it will be the first step to a new order of civilization. It is desirable therefore to look in the face some of the controlling facts which lie behind this cardinal position.

In concentrating attention on the subject of Power, it is necessary for me to ask the reader's attention at this point for a matter which is fundamental. From the beginning of knowledge, the human mind has been exercised in seeking the answer to the question—What is Truth ? Strange as the fact may appear, this question has carried the West into many long eras of stress and violence. Throughout all the changing phases of these periods of development, there has been a position which has never been permitted to present itself in the full light of day to the minds of the combatants, namely, that Truth is inseparably related to Power. Men did not consciously allow themselves to consider this most basal of facts—that in the science of the developing world, Power is the clue not only to human action but to all the principles of knowledge.

The academic system of ideas and arguments about the nature of Truth which the Western mind had reared for centuries was in reality broken to pieces by bringing into sight the actuality which lay behind a statement that formed the heading of one of the chapters of *Social Evolution*. This statement was to the effect that in the social integration *there is no rational sanction for the conditions of progress*. It was the assertion of the essential relationship of Truth to Power, and to Power only, which was expressed in this simple form of words, that constituted the claim to attention. The perception of that relationship sent something like a thrill of re-creation through the dry bones of the philosophies of the West. In the half-articulate period which followed the publication of *Social Evolution*, the leaders of the new movement in Western thought which took the name of Pragmatism, feeling the connexion between

Truth and Power that had been brought into view, ventured hot-foot upon definitions of Truth that swept the builders and definers of dialectic systems of Truth into a state of amazed defence. And well it might be so. For pragmatists began forthwith to define Truth in a way in which the conception of Power alone was visible. They proceeded to define Truth as " That which works " ; " That which is expedient " ; " That which has value " ; and so on.

The time has come when I must respectfully ask pragmatists to give me that right-of-way which is my due. The beginning of this development has not been with them. These definitions of Truth have a lasting value in the history of know-ledge. But they are in the nature of things tentative and incomplete attempts, the natural product of that period of transition which followed the un-covering of the position which I had brought into view. I must in my own way carry this philosophy of Power to the further issues that are involved in it. I, therefore, ask the reader not to be startled if I proceed to give him the answer to the question —What is Truth ? and to follow it up by asserting that it is a complete answer and that the develop-ment of knowledge two thousand years hence, or twenty thousand years hence, will only have served to establish the conviction that it is the final answer.

I. *Truth is the Science of Power.*

To this axiom may be added a second equally fundamental :—

II. *Evolution in all the phenomena of Life follows the line of maximum Power.*

When Christ, claiming to be the exponent of Truth, stood before Pilate's judgment seat, apparently a man utterly beaten and defeated, the cultured Roman asked him the question, " What is Truth ? " Christ, it is recorded, " answered him nothing," so that Pilate marvelled. The position was complete. Nothing could be added to it. For the true answer was utterly beyond Pilate's comprehension. The centre of the greatest Power system which has arisen in history stood before him and he knew it not. For Pilate did not and could not understand the science of Power as it had passed over from the individual to the social integration.

There have been three stages in the definition of the science of Power in the West. In the first stage of it Newton in the *Principia* set forth the laws of the material universe in terms of Force. In the second stage Darwin defined the laws of the individual integration in life in terms of Power.

The third stage is that in which we are now engaged, in which the laws of the social integration in life are being defined similarly in terms of Power.

To understand the application of the doctrine of Power to the current personal and collective activities of the modern world of civilization, it is desirable to have a firm grasp of a few leading principles. The two most essential matters are (1) to understand the distinction to be made between Force and Power; and (2) to understand the nature of the fundamental difference between the controlling law of the individual integration and the controlling law of the social integration.

Now Force and Power are words continually used loosely and often as interconvertible terms in the West.[1] In this chapter, and in future, they will be used by me strictly in the sense in which they are here defined.

Force or Energy is the characteristic or constituent quality of the material universe. Its modes may be changed, but the quantity thereof in the universe cannot be taken from nor added to.

The distinction between Force and Power is fundamental.

[1] Cf. Newton's *Principia*, Introduction to Book III., or the example referred to by Karl Pearson, *Ethic of Free Thought*, p. 32.

III. *Power is the capacity for utilizing Force or Energy by integration—that is to say, by organization,—so as to produce more intense or higher results in one place than would otherwise be possible.*

IV. *Power is the characteristic or constituent quality of life as Force is the characteristic or constituent quality of the material universe.*

V. *Life in all its forms is a process of integration—that is to say, of organization,—of Force or Energy.*

The mind which brought us to the fundamental law of evolution in life as Newton brought us to the fundamental law of the material universe was Darwin's. Darwin and Herbert Spencer gave us the first law of evolution in life in stating the principle which is summarized in the expression *survival of the fittest*, or, in another form, *natural selection*. Both these formulæ have been radically criticized. " To say that to survive is to be the fittest is merely to tell us that to be the fittest is to survive. To say that life progresses by natural selection is merely to tell us that life progresses in the manner in which it does progress." So the criticism has run. Something essential is said to be missing.

As a matter of fact, both formulæ are lacking in an essential element. The axiom or law of progress which supplies what is missing in Darwin's conception and which expresses the characteristic meaning of *integration* in life so as to bring that meaning into line with the principles set out in Book I. of Newton's *Principia* must be put as follows :—

> II. *Integration in life follows the line of maximum Power.*

The principle of the survival of the fittest or natural selection coming to us from Darwin and Spencer is, it will be observed, a less complete expression of this law of maximum Power.

The feature of life is its two phases of integration governed by quite different applications of the law of maximum Power. First, there is the Individual Integration. It was practically with the Individual Integration alone that Darwin was concerned. His conception did not in any real sense extend to the higher or Social Integration. The distinctive governing principle of each of these two phases of evolution may be set out as follows :—

> VI. *In the Individual Integration evolution follows the line of maximum Power through the self-assertion of the individual. The centre of gravity in the process is in the*

> *life of the individual*, i.e., *it is in the present.*

The highest form of Power in the individual integration is that which Darwin described, namely, the highest survival efficiency of those units which are successful in the struggle for their own lives and interests. But—

> VII. *In the Social Integration evolution follows the line of maximum Power through the entire subordination of the lives and welfare of the individual units to a survival efficiency in the social integration which is projected beyond that of the lives and welfare or even the consciousness of the existing units. The centre of gravity in the process is beyond the individual, i.e., it is in the future.*

The highest form of Power in the social integration is that which produces the highest efficiency in securing this type of subordination. I have elsewhere defined this as *Projected Efficiency*.[1]

As we scrutinize closely this statement of the difference between the principles of Power in the individual integration and in the social integration, we have unveiled before us the cause of all the fundamental and deep-seated confusion and conflict in the

[1] *Principles of Western Civilisation*, chap. ii.

standards of the modern West.   *Almost the entire effort of the Western mind to apply Darwinism to the collective standards of the world has been an effort to apply to the affairs of civilization the principles of Power in the individual integration conceiving them to be the principles of Power in the social integration.*   It is evident that the Western mind therein is up against an impossible task.   For Power as expressed through the forms of the social integration is immeasurably greater than Power expressed through the forms of the individual integration of which Darwin gave us the laws.   The principles upon which Power rests in the social integration will therefore be the winning principles in the world.

The ascendant and winning quality in the era of the individual integration has been Reason.   It may be defined as follows :—

> VIII. *Reason is the highest form of the sum of the Self-Regarding emotions.   It is the principal expression of that capacity in mind by which the individual senses the sequences through which Power is related to Force.   It is the chief human organ o, the science of Force.*

Even where reason carries us into the highest regions of practical science, or of thought, or of speculation, its achievements all remain applications

of those winning or survival qualities acquired by
mind in sensing the relations of Force to Power in
the environment out of which man has emerged in
the past.   On the other hand—

The ascendant and winning quality in the era of
the social integration is the Emotion of the Ideal.
This quality may be defined as follows :—

> IX. *The Emotion of the Ideal is the highest
> form of the sum of the Other-Regarding
> emotions.   It is the principal expression
> of that ultra-rational capacity in mind
> through which the individual senses the
> sequences   through   which   individual
> Power   is   related   to   social   Power   in
> higher integration.   It is the chief human
> organ of the science of Power.*

When   these   two   statements   (VIII   and   IX)   are
carefully scrutinized and compared, it will be perceived that there is a far-reaching significance in
the different manner in which Power is transmitted
by heredity in the social integration as compared
with   the   individual   integration.   This   may   be
expressed as follows :—

> X. *In the individual integration the heredity
> through which Power is transmitted is in
> the individual.   It is passed from one
> generation to the next with protoplasmic*

> *continuity. Great change on a large scale is rare and is usually only slowly established.*

It is on this kind of heredity that the attention of science has been almost exclusively concentrated in the past.   As contrasted with it we have in the social integration the following principles :—

> XI. *In the social integration the heredity through which Power is transmitted is in the cultural inheritance.*[1]   *It is independent of protoplasmic continuity. The transmitting agent is the emotion of the ideal. Transforming change on a universal scale can be established quickly, i.e., within the lifetime of a single generation.*

The foregoing axioms carry us to new horizons in Western thought and action.   They form the foundations of the science of Power.   We have to turn now to their practical applications—applications of immeasurable significance in the future of civilization.

[1] See *Social Evolution*, chap. ix., and Sir Edwin Ray Lankester's article " Zoology," *Encyclopædia Britannica*, 11th ed.

CHAPTER VIII

WOMAN IS THE PSYCHIC CENTRE OF POWER IN THE SOCIAL INTEGRATION

FOR long throughout the past human energies have been cramped and limited on every side through the concentration of the Western intellect on the causes which have governed the individual integration as described in the preceding chapter. The mind and will of civilization have been overwhelmingly absorbed in the study of the facts which have made for the efficiency of Power in the struggles of this era. This is a passing phase of the world. The principles of Power in the future all lie in the social integration. And in the social integration the fact of first significance is that Power centres in emotion. The social integration is related in all its phases to that supreme capacity in the collective mind which senses and directs Power, namely, the emotion of the ideal.

One of the strangest facts of our time is this. The West knows practically nothing of the science of emotion. It knows scarcely anything, that is to say, of emotion in its most important manifestations which are in the social integration. If one takes up any of its leading textbooks on psychology at the present time it is to encounter the strange spectacle of every Western writer on the subject, with the prominent exception of Mr. William McDougall and a small group, thinking and theorizing about the facts of emotion almost as if emotion related only to the individual.   Emotion is considered as some relatively inferior quality in the individual closely associated with the animal past and mainly connected with functions which man shares with the animal world.   The science of emotion in its collective aspects is practically a sealed book to the West.

Throughout the stages of the great world war, for instance, it was a matter of daily occurrence, in the Western press and particularly in the press of Great Britain, to see the German peoples contemptuously referred to as the most emotional race in Europe : as if this description at once decisively relegated them to a category of inferiority. Of course the German people were emotional The stupendous lesson in Power which Germany was giving the world was in all its phases and issues a lesson in the illimitable and incalculable

13

power of emotion. Under our prevailing standards in the West we continually think of the control of emotion as if it indicated absence of emotion. So entirely contrary to fact is this misconception that it may be taken as a maxim of civilization that other things being equal, the higher the capacity of any individual or of any people, the higher the capacity for emotion.

It is emotion only which can in its collective applications direct the general mind in the long sequences through which Power must express itself in the social integration. It is through the emotion of the ideal, and through this cause alone, that the collective will can be concentrated and directed over long periods of time to particular ends. It is through emotion only that the present can be subordinated to the future and the organized will of civilization transmitted from one generation to the next through the young. It is through the emotion of the ideal that any collective aim whatsoever that the organized imagination of a people may set before itself in civilization becomes possible of achievement, and this in an incredibly brief interval of time.

Where are we to look for the principal source and reservoir in the future of this supreme capacity ? It will be the seat of all Power. It will be the ultimate cause of dominant efficiency in the coming struggle of the world.

The answer to this question is the most striking which it has ever been the lot of a writer to give. There can be no doubt as to what the reply must be. *It is not in the fighting Male of the race : it is in Woman that we have the future centre of Power in civilization.* This, strange and paradoxical as it may appear, is the first lesson in Power which emerges in history from the great world war of civilization in the second decade of the twentieth century.

If we look at the history of the fighting male of the race in the vast struggle for Power which formed the past history of the world, the significance of certain facts begins to stand out with great distinctness before the mind. The existing world in every phase of its life has been the culminating stage of the prolonged drama of individual efficiency. It is the flowering stage in every institution of the qualities which have made the individuals who are supremely efficient in the struggle for their own interests the centres of all systems of Power and the masters of the world. It represents the age when interests have been short-circuited into the hands of those who have power to hold them by force, and when the instant need of individuals and institutions has been either absolutely or relatively for A to be able to kill B before B is able to kill A.

Now it is evident that in all Power systems in this stage of the human world the fighting male has been, in the nature of things, the ultimate source and origin of supreme Power. He has been the maker, the doer, the creature of the instant and urgent need from the beginning of things. All the qualities based ultimately on his sex have been in the fighting male of the race those of instant realization. It has been the imperious condition of his efficiency in the struggle for Power that there should be no to-morrow in him like to-day. The idealisms of the long sequences, the long-drawn-out dramas of renunciation and sacrifice, have never in reality had more than a pallid meaning for the man of the fighting races of the West.

For this reason there is no practical or business people of the West in which the typical male in his inner heart does not despise idealism and all the characteristic emotion on which idealism rests. At the back of the male mind of every fighting and business people the spirit of the pagan rules and the philosophy of Omar Khayyám is enthroned. In the course of my life, in which my experience has been considerable, I have never known an Englishman who really believed any of the dogmas of the

Christian religion through his reason.   In all cases the individual held to them as part of an inheritance which has been imposed on him from without by causes in which his reason had had no share.

In the integrating systems of Power in the world this basis of things is being swept away.   In the social integration where Power rests on the causes described in the last chapter the story of humanity is becoming with increasing intensity the vast tragic drama of duty, of sacrifice, of renunciation. All the winning systems of Power in the social integration are those in which the centre of gravity is outside the limits of the individual's own consciousness, and in which, in the long sequences of cause and effect, the units are subordinated to a meaning far beyond that of their own lives and interests through the emotion of the ideal.   Reason, in reality, is quite unable to carry any of us from the principles of the individual integration into the principles of the social integration.   The individual dies that the world may live, cannot really be expressed in any terms of the individual's reason. Are you willing to be damned for the glory of God?—is a question which cannot be answered in the affirmative by any process of reason.   But when human nature staggering upwards with its face towards the infinite and universal gives this answer, it has simply reached the highest expression of Power.

These systems of Power in the social integration do not rest on reason. They appeal to no facts—the facts have not arrived. They answer nothing to argument. They are Power itself. They rest on emotion. And through the emotion of the ideal, man therein has hitched himself to omnipotence.

Now if we turn from the fighting male of the race to the other half of the world which is represented in woman, the effect on the mind of these principles is very striking as we begin to perceive their reach. At the back of human consciousness, as the literatures of nearly all peoples bear witness, there has always lurked a conception of woman's mind as being, in circumstances which men have never allowed themselves freely to imagine, a power of incalculable magnitude. Save in the expressions of it, which arise directly out of its relations to the opposite sex, woman's mind at the present time, even in the highest systems of human culture, remains the greatest mystery of the race.

Throughout the whole span of the human era, the development of the mind of woman has represented one fact of absolutely supreme significance, namely, that there has been expressed in it the struggle of the interests of the future against the ascendency in the present of those Power systems, which arise from the activities of the male mind, which rest on force, which by the categorical necessity of the fight must always be directed to sectional and short-range objectives, and which from an outlook thus inherently limited to the need of the present and under the control of reason seek always to impose their own conceptions under the name of the Absolute upon every form of human activity.   These systems of Power, characteristic of the individual integration, have ever sought to exploit woman in all her capacities as no other being has been exploited in life. Out of this struggle the mind of woman has emerged. It is like the emerging mind of civilization itself in the upward stress of progress.   Woman is indeed the actual prototype of all the great systems of religion, of morality, of law, upon which integrating civilization rests.   For in all these the controlling meaning in which their development has centred has been this same struggle for the interests of the future against the systems of force seeking to exploit and overwhelm in the present the interests of the future which were represented in them.

In the individual integration, of which Darwin gave us the laws, the clue to Power in all the qualities and all the institutions of the winning types lies in one fact.   The heredity through which Power is transmitted is in the individual. The centre of gravity in Power is, therefore, in the present. The line of maximum Power which evolution is following is the individual efficient in the struggle for his own interest—the efficient individual, that is to say, whom Nietzsche described to us as acknowledging no authority but his own will and no morality but his own interests. Everything in this individual has been controlled and is still controlled by interests centred in the present, and by the necessity, actual or implicit, in all his institutions for A to be able to kill B before B is able to kill A.

In the social integration the clue to Power is quite different. The heredity through which Power is transmitted is not in the individual. It is the social or cultural inheritance. Evolution continues to follow the line of maximum Power, but it is the characteristic principle of the social integration that immensely greater Power centres in those systems which while remaining efficient in the present at the same time subject the present to the future. The centre of gravity of Power in the social integration is therefore always in the future. The control of the long organized sequences of cause and effect through which evolution thus follows the line of Power in the social integration can be only attained in one way—by emotion directing action through the cultural inheritance over long periods of time to ideals beyond the lives and interests of the existing individuals. *It is woman who, by the necessities of her being, has carried within her nature from the beginning in its highest potentialities the ruling principle of this new era of Power.*

By her history in evolution, by her function in relation to man, by her position in relation to the future generation, woman has ever been the creature of fruition in the future as contrasted with man. The driving principle of woman's nature at all its highest levels has ever been by pure physiological necessity the subjugation of the present with all its imperious demands to a meaning beyond herself and beyond all visible interests in the present. By the necessities of evolution every strand of woman's deeper being has vibrated to this meaning for untold ages. The fighting male is through the nature of his history the creature of those short-range animal emotions which are becoming of less importance in advancing civilization. Woman, on the contrary, through her history has ever been the creature of the long-range emotions through which the instant needs of the present are subordinated to the meaning implicit in the long sequences of cause and effect through which maximum Power expresses itself in the social integration.

Nothing is more surprising to numbers of women who have long worked in public matters in conjunction with men, and also to numbers of men who have had experience of a similar kind in working with women, than the popular impression that woman represents the sex which is liable to be diverted from distant ends by passing emotions, while men are held to be relatively uninfluenced by emotion.   Wide experience almost invariably brings home to the mind that this is the opposite of the truth.   In men all the more powerful emotions are short-range emotions.   They are all, moreover, the emotions intimately related to the overpowering heredity of the fight.   In civilization the necessity for outwardly controlling emotions of this class is constant and imperative.   Men throughout their lives are consequently in constant conflict with their emotions, suppressing them, hiding them, ashamed of them.   The continual object of the male sex in civilization is to appear unemotional, with the result that this pose has become one of the outward marks of culture amongst civilized men.

But this is only on the surface.   The emotions of the male exist beneath in overwhelming strength. Women always by a true and deep-seated instinct despise what they perceive to be the short-range emotions in men in public affairs.   Even in the highest affairs of State, in legal trials, in debating assemblies, the relatively weak emotion of the ideal in man is nearly always a short-range emotion. All displays of eloquence and rhetoric in the male are intimately connected with the emotions of the fight. There is no situation in which a civilized man is so suddenly and so completely transformed into a creature of the short-range emotions of the fight as when he becomes an orator in public affairs. The gesticulations of eloquence, the beating and thumping motions of emphasis, the flashing eye, the excited visage in which the expressions varying from the sublime to the sinister rapidly succeed each other, are all characteristic of early man in the ecstasy of the emotions of the fight.

Lecky has described with striking effect the appearance of Gladstone, with many of the aspects and accompaniments of emotion in the fighting savage, delivering with great eloquence a speech on a high moral cause. I have often seen members of the native fighting races of South Africa, like the Zulus, after drugging themselves with narcotics, wrought up to the highest flights of rhetoric in which suddenly jumping on their feet they deliver to empty space long periods of fiery eloquence and declamation all imbued with the passion and coloured with ideals of the fight.

Even in the service of the highest causes it is the short-range emotion of the fight which most powerfully drives men. I was once present at a private meeting at a crisis in British politics when leaders were being chosen. The name of one leader, now a prominent statesman, was put forward with strong and impressive recommendations by a member present. The most urgent qualification of leadership mentioned was that he was a man capable of reaching any goal in action if only he were excited by the spirit of combativeness, which it was pointed out was powerfully present in the case in question. In pursuit of principles, and in the quests of the intellect in scientific research, it may also be observed continually that it is the emotions inherited from the environment of the hunt, the chase, and the fight which most powerfully operate in the male mind, and this even in the highest regions of abstract knowledge.

As compared with this psychology of the male so strongly developed in all the fighting races of the world, the psychology of woman is absolutely distinct. It is separated from that of man by meanings which are poles apart from those just described. The mind of woman, as we shall see more clearly in the next chapter, has in reality outstripped that of man by an entire epoch of evolution in the development of those characteristic qualities upon which Power now rests in the social integration.   Nearly all the past discussions about woman may be perceived at a glance to be occupied with aspects of the case which have no important relation to the fundamental issue with which we are about to become involved in civilization.   Man has been engaged in discussing woman in the past from the point of view of woman's case with man or of man's case with woman.   But civilization is not ultimately concerned in a fundamental way with either of those issues.   The central problem is the relation of woman, not to man, but to the needs of society.

In this matter developing civilization is being driven by causes which are inherent in a direction which is inevitable.   Evolution will follow the line of maximum Power.   It is this question of Power which will ultimately control everything.   And the significant fact towards which we have to turn is that the qualities through which maximum Power must express itself in the long sequences of the social integration, the qualities, that is to say, for which civilization cries aloud now with the living hunger of a type in evolution, are precisely those which are most characteristically represented in the mind of woman.   They are the qualities by which woman instinctively subjects the present to the future through sustained emotion, accompanied by a power of sacrifice in the service of the ideal which greatly exceeds this capacity in the male sex.

When we turn for the case about woman from this point of view of Power the facts deeply impress the imagination. It is well to put entirely aside all the comparisons upon which the popular mind has run in the past of woman's capacities with man's capacities at the level of man's standards—strength, endurance, brain qualities, work capacities, character inheritance—all the comparisons of these qualities in woman with man's standards with which we have been usually occupied have no real significance.

Woman's relationship to Power is so different from man's in the social integration that it is at present almost beyond the full comprehension of the male mind.

To get the matter into focus it is better to avoid all preconception arising from the past, and to do this most thoroughly it is better not to take the case for woman in relation to civilization from any of its advocates, but to go straight to the discussions about woman's sex and woman's mind which have been carried on by those who have put the case against woman in civilization in the most thoroughgoing manner and in the most extreme spirit of hostility.

The whole modern attack in the West on woman's mind and the qualities of her sex centres primarily in Schopenhauer.[1] The most savage but also the most reasoned and influential case that has been made against woman in the literature of the West has come from Schopenhauer. In his oft-quoted essay on woman Schopenhauer represents, as nobody else either in literature or in science does, the cry of the inmost heart of the pagan of the West who has built the world of the individual integration on force. Nearly all the current arguments against woman's position find their best statement in this essay. Even the crude, fierce, animal attacks on woman in later literature, like those of Nietzsche, Weiniger, and others which have followed them, are scarcely more than echoes of Schopenhauer. Their point of view is best studied in Schopenhauer's essay, where the essential positions are made with greater strength and moderation.

The first thing which strikes the observer of insight on reading Schopenhauer's essay is that Schopenhauer's mind, in the contemplation of woman, is revealed to the reader in a state of fear.

[1] Schopenhauer's Essay on Woman, Belfort Bax's volume of Selections.

The essay exhibits the dread of woman's mental influence as a kind of overwhelming obsession of Schopenhauer's intellect, just as the fear of woman's physical influence is exhibited in the early patristic writings as an overwhelming obsession of the ascetic mind.   It will be perceived clearly at a later period that the mental attitude of Schopenhauer in this case is characteristically true to type.   The psychology of Schopenhauer in the essay is the typical psychology of Power recognizing its true relation to Power, which it fears to be destined to supersede it.

Schopenhauer's central position is extraordinarily fundamental and uncompromising.   He declares woman to be the natural enemy of man.   The reason given for thus describing her has to be noted.   She is, he asserted, the breaker and subduer of man's will power.   We recognize on scrutiny that this will power which Schopenhauer has in mind is none other than the will power of the fighting male of the race—the terrible, all-subduing, dominant creature of efficiency in the individual integration, acknowledging no authority but his own will and no morality but his own advantage.   And it is as the representative of this dominant will power of the past that we see Schopenhauer standing before woman in a state of instinctive and almost vindictive intellectual hostility. His description of her in such remarkable circumstances reads almost like a hymn of hate.

Schopenhauer forthwith describes woman as inherently a creature of evil. Her relations to life have made of her, he said, an inborn liar. He declares her to be an intellectual myope. He describes her fundamental failings to be injustice, treachery, and deception. He asserts her to be wanting in all objectivity of mind. He will not allow her the conditions of originality. She is, he said, below the male standard in intellect. He even denies woman's sex beauty. It was only, he said, the male intellect of humanity when befogged through the sexual impulse which could consider the female sex fair.

Moved by his emotions thus to curse woman altogether, Schopenhauer advances immediately to one of the most remarkable positions in the history of thought. Driven by the true instinct of genius, Schopenhauer in the same essay proceeds to write woman's charter of authority for al ages in the future of civilization. For the cause of all the qualities, which he has thus enumerated as making of woman a creature to be dreaded, Schopenhauer puts down the one significant cause. The root quality of evil in woman Schopenhauer declares to be this. *The*

14

race is always to her more than the individual. The natural, the inborn, and the unchanging attitude of the whole of woman's sex to man Schopenhauer asserts to be the attitude of woman to an all-powerful opponent whose strength to enforce his will has to be subdued to a purpose in the future. For in the darkest recesses of their hearts, he continues, "women live altogether more in the race than in the individual; they regard the affairs of the species as more serious than those of the individual." [1]

It is this extraordinary insight into woman's true relationship to Power which constitutes Schopenhauer's main contribution to the sum of human knowledge. In the result it drives him into a kind of frenzied opposition to woman. The line of Schopenhauer's successors in the modern West have since consistently striven to develop the doctrine of Power with their faces set resolutely to the past, until it becomes at length in the individual and in the state alike the disastrous Nietzschean doctrine of strength acknowledging no authority but its own will and no morality but its own advantage. Of Woman, said Nietzsche, "Thou goest to her: do not forget thy whip." [2] Of the State, said Bernhardi, "the whole discussion turns not on international

[1] *Op. cit.,* p. 343.   [2] *Zarathustra.*

right but simply and solely on power and expediency." [1]

Yet it was the same Schopenhauer who, standing at the head of the great modern pagan retrogression thus indicated, visualized woman as its natural and invincible antagonist. It is Schopenhauer who has given us woman's charter for all time in civilization. As distinct from man she is *the creature to whom the Race is more than the Individual, the being to whom the Future is greater than the Present.* Let civilization remember it.

When we turn now to the practical affairs of civilization and try to focus the light of this principle on the facts of the world, the illumination will be found to extend to a great distance. The evidence for the statement that it is woman by reason of her functional, racial, and evolutionary history who is the principal organ in the race of that emotion of the ideal upon the function of which developing civilization depends, is of great extent and significance.

In the integrating systems of civilization Power, as we have seen, is not transmitted through the heredity of the individual but through the cultural or social inheritance. To be able to direct or control this social heredity through the emotion of the ideal is to be able in a relatively brief period to

[1] *Germany and the Next War.*

alter or profoundly modify the world or any of its existing institutions. It is to obtain control over all the reservoirs of Power in civilization. The relationship of woman to the cultural heredity of the world through the emotion of the ideal is therefore the first fact which meets us on the threshold of the science of Power.

The emotion of the ideal is an inseparable and the most essential part of that capacity in the human mind which senses Power. Woman from her history in the past in subjection to force has doubtless from an early period possessed this capacity in a high degree. It is peculiar to her now that under more complete conditions of civilization she possesses, in a far higher state of development than it has reached in man, the sense which instinctively recognizes the sequences through which Power is transmitted in the social integration. Power in the social integration, as Spencer long ago pointed out, resides in those causes which produce the long sequences of effect as contrasted with the motives and impulses which in savagery produce the less important, rapid and short-range effects. It is not in the nature of things that the male who has been from the beginning the doer, the maker, the builder, the fighter, the instrument of force, the attendant on all the instant need of things in the present, should be the equal of woman in this quality of subordinating the present to the future by the emotion of the ideal.

It is a circumstance which has to be noted that amongst the advanced fighting races this fact is nearly always instinctively recognized by men. Almost every male of the Western races, as soon as he becomes involved in the activities of Power which are characteristic of the social integration, has the same instinct. When he has need of the emotion of the ideal to carry him beyond the thick of his present difficulties, or beyond the outlook of his environment, or into these higher regions of leadership which require sacrifice prolonged beyond all interests of the present, he turns instinctively, not to another male of his kind, but to woman for support and instinctive understanding.

Men tend to hide this characteristic from their fellows in a world in which the standards of the individual integration still survive in great strength. But it is developed to the highest and completest extent in the leading and strongest minds. One has to turn to such records as Moltke's love letters and his letters to his wife to see to what an extent minds which in the popular imagination have represented the personification of power—power precise, calculating, methodical, mathematical—

have possessed this characteristic. Power in minds of the highest calibre is nearly always thus exhibited as in the closest association with the emotion of the ideal. And in such circumstances when we know the facts we see them turning instinctively and naturally to woman to give strength to that quality in them which is the principal element in Power in its highest expressions.

It is characteristic of woman that the habit of mind required in these circumstances is nearly always present. It is generally inborn even though it remain latent. It renders members of the sex capable of attaining over long stretches of time a lofty, permanent, and controlled excitement which exercises a profound influence over all the activities of ordinary life. It is this kind of capacity which enables even delicate women to maintain constancy to an ideal for a prolonged period in the face of the greatest difficulties and persecutions. Women in such circumstances have the same capacity for devotion to causes as they have in other circumstances to persons even through a long succession of mental and bodily tortures. J. S. Mill described the type of mind from which this quality proceeds either in man or woman as always closely associated with the power of leadership of mankind.[1]

[1] *Subjection of Women*, chap. iii. §11.

It is one of the strongest and most fundamental traits of woman's nature closely associated with this quality that in a conflict between present interest and principle she instinctively and instantly tends to take the side of principle rather than that of interest. It is in the possession of this characteristic that woman is in high degree actually and literally what Schopenhauer described her to be, namely, the being to whom the race is more than the individual and the future greater than the present. It is in such circumstances that Schopenhauer correctly estimated her as the enemy to be dreaded by the strong man acknowledging no authority but his own will and no morality but his own advantage ; because, to use his words, " always with woman the spring of her secret, unexpressed, and indeed unconscious and inborn morality, is the belief that the welfare of the species is placed in her hands."[1] Woman is, in short, by nature the custodian of ends distant in the future to which she subdues the present : so that, again to use Schopenhauer's words, " in the recesses of her heart she lives always and altogether more in the race than in the individual."[1]

These facts possess a significance of a high order when their relationship to the science of Power as directed through the cultural inheritance of

[1] Schopenhauer's Essay on Woman, *op. cit.*

civilization is distinguished. There is no more remarkable phenomenon of the modern Western world than that vast change, now in progress in the psychology of the race, which has a bearing intimately related to this subject.

In the literature of imagination and idealism it is impossible to ignore certain features. In the imaginative literature of the peoples of the modern West as contrasted with the literature of peoples of more primitive times and standards, a fact which strikes the mind is the position occupied therein by woman. She stands out as the central figure. It is woman who inspires nearly all the deeds, and nearly all the deep passions of men, which form the subject of the imaginative literature of the modern races. Even under the fiercest practical and competitive aspects of life we do not escape from the presence of this fact. The imaginative literature of the West is the vehicle in one form or another of all its highest idealisms. But it is woman who is always in evidence therein as the touchstone of man's ideals. Wherever man becomes an idealist in imaginative literature it is almost invariably woman who is the measure of it. It is to the woman that man always brings his idealisms to prove them and to look for support.

So deep seated is this instinct that it has become

one of the most fundamental canons of modern
Western Art, that it cannot be violated without a
sense of failure being created.   Wherever man is
represented in Art as the higher idealist and woman
as the lower cause which has dragged him down the
result is artistic disaster.   We feel that the ideal
has been lowered and that we have returned to the
depressing atmosphere of a more primitive stage
of human evolution.   However great the ability
or the genius of the creator it cannot save us from
this effect.   As in Robert Herrick's *The Healer*, or
as in George Gissing's *New Grub Street*, the result is
invariably the same.   A sense of failure and outrage
is present in the mind of the reader.

It has to be kept in view in considering this
significant transition in the standards of Art that
in the present epoch of the world woman's mind is
the greatest mystery of the time.   In the stunting
and restraining conditions of the era out of which it
has emerged it has been driven in upon itself at
every point to such an extent that the world knows
scarcely anything about it, save in those expressions
of it which arise directly out of woman's relations
to the opposite sex.

The most notable and probably unforeseen effect
on many Western minds of Pierre Loti's *Désen-
chantées*, which produced so remarkable an im-

pression in the harems of Turkey, was to bring home to those minds to a degree never before experienced the peculiar and intensely restricted relationship of woman to the general world, not simply in Eastern harems but throughout the whole of Western civilization at the present day.

The qualities of the male mind inherited from lower levels of evolution have been ennobled and transmuted at higher levels with enormous effect in the service of civilization. Not so has it been in the case of the mind of woman. The effect of woman's entire education, and of the social training which accompanies it down to the present day in civilization, has been to shut off to an incalculable degree the characteristic and peculiar inherent values of her mind from access to the service of civilization. The culminating effect in the past of the attitude of civilization to woman even amongst the most advanced peoples has been to inculcate the doctrine that the only duty which woman owes to the world is that which she owes through those to whom she is related through the sexual bond. Her deeper and more characteristic nature has been prevented as much by Western usage as by Eastern from being released into any other channel than that of her husband and her family.

Yet even in such conditions in which the access of woman's mind to the larger world of affairs has been walled up at all the principal approaches the results have been remarkable. It is one of the most pregnant facts in the upward progress of the race that the emotion of the ideal in its relation to Power has *always* had its chief and deepest expressions in the mind of woman. Even with all the disabilities under which her sex has laboured, woman's mind in the past has been the principal source of the creative idealism of the world. When all other channels have been closed to her, woman has carried the creative capacity of the emotion of the ideal into the practical world of affairs mainly through her influence on the mind of the young. She has done this to an extent of which a large part of the world is quite unconscious.

If it were possible in periods of unusual growth and crisis in the history of the world to uncover the foundations of events and to get a view of causes and origins, it would be found that the creative and sustaining influence of woman's mind in the formative stages preceding action is enormous. A knowledge of the methods by which the standards and ideas of the time are imposed on successive generations of men leaves no doubt that the influence of woman on the cultural inheritance has equalled and probably far exceeded that of all other agencies whatever.

The effect of the emotion of the ideal transmitted to the young of the rising generation by woman can never after be entirely effaced in the individual. It is greater, deeper, and more enduring than the effect of any system whatever of subsequent education. Where it is combined with the effects of such subsequent education, as to some extent it is in the systems of modern Germany and Japan, it becomes the most powerful element in character formation, giving after results in capacity for permanent and sustained aim and sacrifice in the individual absolutely impossible of attainment by any other means.

Wide acquaintance with the personal memoirs of men who have been centres of Power in history, who have become leaders of causes, or who have given direction to the idealisms of classes, of interests, or of nations or of peoples in civilization, leave developed in the mind with great strength the conviction that the part played by woman in giving direction to the mind of the young through the emotion of the ideal far exceeds that imagined by the world. It has been one of the principal determining factors throughout human history.

Knowledge of the influence which it is capable of exercising has been the basis of many potent systems of education. But it has been knowledge which has fallen far short of the reality. To measure the influence of woman in shaping and determining the mind of civilization through the young in the past is possible only to the most experienced minds. It has extended even to the regions of the highest abstract thought. Leslie Stephen, in reviewing the history of philosophical systems, gave it as his own experience that however honestly and eagerly the philosopher may desire to try his conclusions by the severest test, always in the end his real problem came to be : " How conclusions which are agreeable to his emotions can be connected with the postulates which are congenial to his intellect."[1]   That is to say, in short, that it is always the emotion of the ideal which predetermines the conclusions.

And in nearly all such cases when the inquiry is carried far enough, the significant controlling fact in the background is found to be that the emotion of the ideal has had its strength and direction given to it by the influence of woman's mind at an early stage in the development of the individual.

All the foregoing results, and they are of the

[1] *The English Utilitarians*, vol. i.

highest order of significance to the existing world, have been under the conditions of the past when woman has been practically without any contact, in her own right or in the right of her sex, with the living facts of the real world of human activities. They open to the mind a vision of possibilities of the science of Power of which men have not dreamed. A new horizon in the history of Power will be reached in the world when civilization perceives the significance of utilizing towards the aims of collective Power this being to whom, through the emotion of the ideal, the race is always more than the individual and the future greater than the present. The type of civilization which first organizes itself around this central capacity of woman's mind will have a stupendous advantage over all others in the coming struggle of the world.

CHAPTER IX

THE MIND OF WOMAN

IT has been said in the last chapter that in the background of human consciousness there has always been present the conception of woman's mind as being, in circumstances which men have not allowed themselves to imagine, a power of incalculable magnitude. This conception is visible in the records of many primitive peoples. It is to be found in later Roman history; it was in evidence for a brief space in the second and third centuries, from the period of Gaius onward, when woman, at the height of Roman civilization, having with the assistance of the legal mind emerged from the restrictions of *manus*, attained to a position of almost complete independence and the equality of the sexes was assumed by Roman jurisconsults as a fundamental principle of equity.

The same fact is to be witnessed strongly presenting itself in various forms in modern times. The violent dislike and distrust of woman shown by the crowd of writers, and later by many men of action, who have followed Schopenhauer and Nietzsche, in imagining the winning principles of Power in the Individual Integration to be the winning principles of Power in the Social Integration, are in reality a striking tribute to the mind of woman. For what has to be recognized therein is that the fear of woman's mental influence is exhibited as a kind of overwhelming obsession of the male intellect. Even the more reasoned opposition to the claims of the sex, often encountered in the current world in persons of the highest ideals, is to be taken as testimony to the underlying perception of the reach of woman's powers. For in the case of most persons of this class, especially those of the strongest convictions and sincerity, it is the instinct of the enormous potential influence of woman's mind in the coming order of civilization which drives them to oppose with all their might attempts to employ that influence in what they conceive to be a wrong and misguided manner.

In dealing with the mind of woman in the future of civilization the fundamental fact that must ever be kept clearly in view is the relationship of woman to Power. Scarcely any of the writers of social science textbooks have yet grasped the full significance of this relationship, and of the fact that the clue to all events and to all principles in the future is that Power in the highest form of integration will win.

Now the highest form of Power in the social integration is that in which society is rendered organic to the highest possible degree. Almost the only object to which society as a whole has been collectively organized in the past has been the object of successful war directed to the smashing and conquest of other peoples or to resistance against such an attempt. There has been no example hitherto in the world of Power in its highest and supreme type, that is to say, in a society in which mind has been organized and steadily directed through all the forms and functions of civilization over an indefinite number of generations towards the attainment of an ideal conceived to embrace the highest and the whole meaning of human effort. It is this type of society which is inevitable in the future of the world; for in the struggle for survival it will exceed in Power all other types. But to organize Power in this supreme type is possible in society in one way only. The existing individuals must be rendered capable of subordinating their minds, their lives, and all the interests within the span of their lives, to an ideal which is beyond their

15

lives, and which may even at times be beyond their understanding.

In this deeply organized type of society efficiency projected thus into the future always of necessity implies and includes efficiency in the present. A society which is capable of consistently subordinating the present to the future has within it the power of realizing practically any aim which it may set before itself in civilization. The social mind directed forward with great strength and unity over long stretches of time to an ideal end held in view is a force absolutely irresistible. The political systems of Power organized in this way will win out over all others in the struggle of the world in the future.

The cause which makes these higher systems of Power possible has been designated in these chapters the *emotion of the ideal*. Many years ago William James graphically described in the first edition of his *Textbook of Psychology* the manner in which this cause of illimitable Power mainly represented in the mind of woman works in the individual. He did not call the cause the emotion of the ideal. He did not deal with its transmission through the social heredity, or with its wide effects as related to Power as I have discussed these matters here. But within the limits that confine it, James's descrip-

tion of the manner in which the emotion of the
ideal works in the mind of the individual is complete
and of the first importance. There is enshrined
within me, as within every one of us, says James,
an inner man. This inner or real man he describes
to be the ideal social or other-regarding self. " It
may be remote," he continues, "it may be represented
as barely possible. I may not hope for its realization
during my lifetime. I may even expect the future
generations, which would approve of me if they
knew me, to know nothing about me when I am
gone. Yet still the emotion which beckons me on
is indubitably the pursuit of an ideal social self." [1]
James proceeds then to analyse the workings of this
cause in the mind of the individual almost up to the
point at which we begin to be concerned with its
collective function as the vehicle of illimitable Power.

"What is the nature of the ideal social self ? "
asks James. The reply is to the effect that it is
a self which seeks to set up within the individual
nothing less than the standards of Universal Mind.
They are the same standards of Absolute or Universal
Mind which we attribute to God. It is characteristic of this inner self that, to quote James's words,
" it can find its adequate *socius* only in an ideal
world." All social progress, he continues, consists

[1] *Text Book of Psychology,* ch. xii,

in the substitution of higher standards for lower; and it is the distinctive quality of this inner tribunal that it sets up the highest standard of all—that of Universal Mind. "Most men," he concludes, " either continually or occasionally carry a reference to it in their breast. The humblest outcast on this earth can feel himself to be real and valid by means of this higher recognition."

It is in making the standards of this other-regarding self the basis of the social inheritance, and in the organization and transmission of this inheritance under the influence of the emotion of the ideal, that there lies the road to the attainment of any object that a people may set before itself. Once the influence of the ideal is imposed upon the individual by social heredity, as described in Chapter V, he can never escape from it. It is this creation of the ideal, and the organization of the minds upon which it is imposed into the collective will, that constitute the first objective in the science of Power in the future of the world.

From time immemorial the interests in which Power has expressed itself through the self-regarding emotions have imposed their will on the world. The systems of Power, acknowledging no law and no morality but their own advantage, to which the interests resting on self have given rise, have organized themselves until they have filled the world in the past with the stress and fury of their activities. But never hitherto have the higher systems of Power which rest on the other-regarding emotions organized themselves throughout civilization with similar intensity, determined to obtain control of the social inheritance and determined to impose on the world the ideals which they have the power of realizing in civilization.

In considering the principles of Power in its highest forms, the significance and the reach in the era that is before us of the principles of the inner mind of woman become now more clearly visible. As soon as we perceive the character of the conditions assembled in the world it is evident that all systems of political utilitarianism founded on self-interest, such as those which Bentham, the Mills, and Herbert Spencer helped to build up in Britain, and all the systems of military utilitarianism in which self is glorified, as in the system which modern Germany sought to establish in the West, must pass in time to the rubbish-heap. Their final condemnation lies in the fact that, despite all appearance to the contrary, *they have no ultimate validity as systems of Power*. As soon as civilization knows its own mind and perceives its own objective, with the means and instruments to attain it, it will be perceived, strange as it may appear, that these systems have not a chance in the long run in the stern struggle of the world. They will all go down in the end before the long-range, long-sequence, integrating systems of Power of which the meaning transcends self and all the interests of self, of which the centre of gravity is always in the future and of which the history in all the stages constitutes that vast, tragic, ennobling, world-building drama of subordination and duty resting on sacrifice. These are the systems organized in the highest degree and therefore powerful in the highest degree, towards which life by the laws inherent in it must evolve in the social integration.

To the evolutionist who understands his subject and who has once firmly grasped in all its bearings the leading fact that the science of evolution is the science of Power, the conclusion suggested in these chapters begins here to present itself with great strength as a conviction. He sees clearly that the part which he has played in the past will not remain to the fighting male. It is the mind of woman which is destined to take the lead in the future of civilization as the principal instrument of Power.

It will be recognized in time as a fact beyond dispute that it is in the mind of woman that there is reached the completest expression of the sum of the other-regarding emotions which has been defined throughout these chapters as the emotion of the ideal.   Schopenhauer spoke with an insight in advance of all the philosophers and reasoners of his century when he described woman as the being of the race rather than of the individual.   It is woman who, in the long æons of evolutionary stress out of which her mind has emerged, has ever been, by reason of her relations to the man on the one hand, and to the next generation on the other, the creature in the constitution of whose mind, to a far greater extent than in the case of the mind of a man, the interests of the future, the distant, and the universal have been represented.   She has lived continually in every kind of motive and emotion driving her to express herself in others and to subordinate the present to the future.

The struggle of woman with Power for untold ages has thus been a struggle which has gradually brought her mind far closer to the principles of the universal mind than the mind of man.   It is for this reason that, as we saw in the last chapter, woman naturally and instinctively subordinates interest to principle. The secret of man's progress is that he has gradually released into the service of civilization, ever at higher and higher levels, all the stern qualities of the chase and the fight bred in him through long ages of primitive struggle.   But when the emotion of the ideal in woman, similarly bred in her through the long stages of our primitive past, is in like manner released into the service of civilization, the effect will transcend the effect of man's qualities. Woman as a sex will reveal in these circumstances the same power of devotion to ideals, to causes, as she does to persons. Her relationship to the future through the long eras of her evolution in the past has permanently endowed woman's mind with a capacity for self-sacrifice and renunciation, persisting through every variety of opposition and of suffering even to death, which is the highest product of the other-regarding emotions, and which in woman is without any superior example in the whole realm of mind.

The elemental hunger of civilization at the present moment is for a public opinion able to subordinate the present to the future—for a public opinion, that is to say, which would express through the collective will just the qualities which are here described as reaching in woman their highest expression. By no other means than this can civilization secure to itself the capacity to rise above the rule of the systems of Power, knowing no law but their own interests, namely, than by a public opinion which is touched with and sustained by emotion in the manner described in Chapter V. The miracle which was related in that chapter as taking place in every lifetime in the will of the individual, when he is made to pass irrevocably into another world by the influence on him of the internal standards set up in his mind through the cultural inheritance, is a miracle which under proper conditions is bound to be wrought equally in the collective will.

This direction of the collective will through the cultural inheritance to definite ends over long stretches of time has become the most urgent need of civilization. *But the fact of the age which goes deeper than any other is that the male mind of the race, as the result of the conditions out of which it has come, is by itself incapable of rendering this service to civilization.* It is in the mind of woman that the winning peoples of the world will find the psychic centre of Power in the future.

The immense importance of the function of the cultural heredity of civilization imposed on the mind of the young of each generation under the influence of the emotion of the ideal was described in Chapter V. It is the most pregnant fact in the history of Power as written in the struggles of modern peoples. Any end towards which the will of civilization is directed in this manner has become possible of attainment. Any existing institution of the world can be altered or transformed in a brief period.

The bearing of these facts has already become visible to the occupying interests in civilization. Under a multitude of aspects it has become the chief aim of the interests which have ruled in the past to move the world now through the organization of opinion and to enlist the emotion of the ideal in the service of their own schemes of Power.

But this to the occupying interests of the past is an infinitely difficult task. For these interests cannot enlist this quality, nor maintain it, nor inspire it, except at its lowest levels. It is an important fact that it has never been possible in history to organize on a large scale and to steadily direct over long periods of time to a clearly defined end in the service of civilization the emotion of the ideal at its highest potentiality. The reason has been that it has not been possible hitherto to carry the emotion of the ideal into action on a universal scale except through the male mind. Civilization has therefore never been able to enlist in its service at the highest level of possible achievement this capacity of mind. The chief reservoir of it as it exists in the race is in the mind of woman, and it has never been uncovered. This is the most significant fact in the science of Power.

It may be observed that it is this struggle between the characteristic standards of mind that express themselves in man, and the characteristic standards of mind that express themselves in woman, which has come to dominate all the leading activities of civilization. The overwhelming heredity of the fight compels every form of Power expressing itself through men, and particularly through men of the Western races, towards that objective of self-realization in the present which is distinctive of the male mind. All the standards of conduct to the influence of which war is due are essentially standards of the self-regarding emotions thus driving men to self-realization in the present. "There are no Rights in the world like Mine." "There are no People in the world like Us." "There is no To-morrow in the world like To-day." These are the cries which have from the beginning represented the elemental emotions underlying war. They carry a challenge to the primary law of civilization with its centre of gravity in the future as deep seated as is the challenge of the highwayman to the first law of ordered society.

Nothing can ever reconcile this elemental antagonism between the principles of civilization and the principles of war. One side must ultimately annihilate the other. But no material or economic cause, no agreement between nations, can in itself abolish war. War can never be brought to an end until the cultural inheritance of civilization imposed on each generation from childhood onwards under the influence of the emotion of the ideal renders it as impossible for a nation to engage in war and lose that principal motive of self-respect which makes life worth living as it is now impossible for the normal civilized man, apart from any question whatever of material loss or gain or punishment, to engage in robbery or murder.

It is one of the most remarkable facts of human nature that the emotion of the ideal, which is the sum and highest form of the other-regarding emotions, is hardly represented at all in the male mind when the wide and particularly the future interests of civilization are concerned. Alike in the history of its external State policy and in the history written in its own statute books, nearly every Western country bears witness to this fact. The spirit of the saying noted by Durkheim as attributed to the Emperor of Germany, that, " For me, humanity ends at the Vosges," [1] is not peculiar to any country. It is the true inborn spirit of the heredity of the fighting male of the West coming down from ages before the dawn of history.

The inability to subordinate the present to the future is a pronounced characteristic of civilization

[1] *Germany above All*, p. 23.

under the rule of the male mind. While Western countries, in order to carry on war, have drawn mortgages on the future which stagger the imagination, there had not arisen up to the date of the world war of 1914 any democracy which possessed the power of subordinating itself to an ideal in the future even to the limited extent of paying off its national debt in times of peace in the interests of posterity. The lack of this capacity to conceive the importance of the future is visible in nearly all public and class movements in the West. How many workmen, asks a living writer, with the object of reducing all such idealisms to absurdity, would refuse an annuity of £200 a year on the chance that by doing so he might raise the rate of wages 1 per cent 300 years hence? The more practical the nation, the more successful the class of men in the struggle for their own interests, the more absurd does such a standard of renunciation appear to them.

As soon as we get down to the realities which lie behind the science of Power in civilization, it will be perceived that in all that pertains to the emotion of the ideal at those higher levels at which it is most powerfully capable of influencing public opinion in sustained effort directed to an objective beyond the present, the mind of woman has in reality already outstripped the mind of the male of the race by an entire era of evolution. It is not without significance that in the four principal forms of activity through which public opinion in the West is influenced most directly and on the largest scale, namely, in art, literature, philosophy, and religion, all the principal revolutionary and developmental movements in recent times have a common meaning which is related to this fact. They are all best summed up as movements which represent the effort of the male mind to reach consciously, through slow, laborious, and - painful stages and by an entirely different road, the position which is already woman's by inborn inheritance.

In the recent leading article, the *Times*, in commenting on a letter of Sir Martin Conway in its columns, called attention to a remarkable change which has been silently taking place under our eyes over a long period in the standards of art in the West.[1] The chief aspect of this change was pointed out to consist in the fact that, to summarize Sir Martin Conway's words, we are gradually losing sense of all the formative arts (meaning thereby arts like painting and sculpture) as a means of expression, the products of such arts coming to be regarded merely as decorative objects ; while, on the other hand, the greatest living art of

[1] *Times*, 23 March 1914.

the present is tending more and more to find its expression in literature and similar mediums through which the world is being powerfully moved by the creation of opinion.

Now the clue to development in art, as in all other. forms of human activity, is the underlying relationship to Power. The beginning and end of the meaning inherent in art is capable of being expressed in a single word—Emotion. All art is nothing else than the capacity of rendering emotion contagious and so of becoming an instrument of Power by influencing human action. The history of development in art is, therefore, the history of the development in the artist of the power of rendering emotion contagious at various levels, as mind in evolution gradually rises from the standpoint of the individual in the self-regarding emotions to the standpoint of the universal in the other-regarding emotions. This is the fundamental law of progress in art and it is identical in meaning with the fundamental law of progress in ethics.

What, then, is the significance of the transition in current Western art described by Sir Martin Conway, for in it we are called to witness the products of the formative arts like sculpture and painting declining from the function of living art and coming to be regarded merely as decorative objects, while the greatest art of to-day is tending to find its expression in literature and similar mediums?

The true answer to this question carries us far. It is doubtless to this effect. The characteristic art of the West in the past, which has expressed itself through formative mediums like sculpture and painting, is the art of the era of the ascendancy in the world of the fighting male. It is, therefore, art which, as Tolstoy with profound intuition perceived, is essentially pagan in character.[1] It is the art of which Grant Allen tried to give, and in large measure succeeded in giving us, the true Darwinian principles in his *Physiological Æsthetics*. In it there is expressed, over and above everything else, the feelings and emotions through which the individual was rendered successful in the struggle for his own interests, and through which the individual, thus successful, became the dominant power in creation. The formative art of the West is, in short, the art of all the world which most profoundly expresses the pyschology of the male.

That the essentially male psychology of the formative arts of the West, which glorifies the self-regarding emotion under every aspect, is the cause which directs and rules the artist in all his efforts, may be observed on every hand. The reflective

[1] *What is Art?* p. 161 et seq.

observer who walks through the ancient sculptures in the Grecian and Roman galleries of the British Museum, and who then carries his mind to the similar effects reproduced in modern statuary in the open spaces and public buildings of London, will have this impression bred immovable within him. He will have it confirmed and reinforced in an unmistakable manner by an extended study of the art of Europe as it is expressed in sculpture in almost every Western city.

The effect aimed at in the art of statuary is everywhere the same throughout the West. In groups without number of classical and sham-classical statues and effigies the sustained effort in sculpture is to glorify or deify almost every human attribute through which the self-regarding emotions can be expressed in their most intense form. Representations of athletes, winged figures, helmeted warriors, dying heroes; representations of struggles, duels, rapes, battles; representations of youths, men, women, crowds, animals; representations, in short, of power and mastery in every position and adventure are intended to make contagious admiration for the qualities through which the self-regarding emotions can be expressed at their highest power.

This spirit has reached in Europe in the cities of modern Prussia a peculiar efflorescence, which has been contemporaneous with the development in Germany of the intellectual and military standards described in previous chapters. A recent writer,[1] describing the remarkable effects to be witnessed in a view of the Schlossbruecke and Museum at Berlin, recapitulates the enormous number of groups and the attitudes portrayed. " To crown everything," he continues, " and to introduce strikingly the Prussian symbol, above the plinth of the main entrance of the Museum are no fewer than eighteen representations of the Prussian eagle. Thus, on a space of ground represented by a frontage of what cannot be much more than fifty yards, there are to be seen no fewer than forty-nine classical representations in stone of one attribute or personality and another." The dominant aim in all the effects, whether represented thus or on a less ambitious scale, scarcely ever varies. Expressed in sculpture in all its forms in the West, this aim is to typify the self-regarding emotions and to portray them triumphing in the most perfect living instruments of force.

In the sister art of painting, the underlying influence is not so visible at first sight. But the discriminating mind soon perceives that the in-

[1] F. M. Hueffer, *When Blood is their Argument*, Part III. chap. i. § vi.

fluence of the same dominating male psychology pervades all its expressions. It may be distinguished how it penetrates to details, even in an art like landscape painting. " How the æsthetic value of a picture of a wood is enhanced," says Schopenhauer, the typical pagan of the West, " if the artist paints, as he should, a solitary pine standing out above the others, high and erect towards heaven." Why? Because, in the formative arts of the West, the meaning which the artist seeks to utter always springs from a subconscious psychology which is profoundly male. Unconsciously the fighting mind realizes and revels in every feature and detail which suggest to it the omnipotence of force. In the detail of the solitary pine standing out high and erect towards heaven, it translates into contagious emotion the symbol of power thus portrayed as conquering gravity.

This tendency in art is in conflict with the deepest and most characteristic evolutionary tendency underlying Western civilization. All the leading movements in modern art, from Pre-Raphaelism to Post-Impressionism and Futurism, reflect phases of the meaning of the struggle between these two forces engaged. The monstrous inspiration which Western art inherited from the ancient civilizations was that of the self-regarding emotions triumphing through the perfection of the living instruments of force. The formative arts have been the chief mediums through which this inspiration has been interpreted.

But the inspiration which underlies all the forward movements in the civilization of our time, is that of the triumph of the other-regarding emotions through the belief that the life of the individual is related to ends and principles which transcend in importance every present interest in the world around us.

It is for this reason that the tendency in our time is for the greatest art of the day to become more and more what may be termed invisible art. The highest art is, therefore, seeking to express itself in the mediums through which the emotion of the ideal, which, it must be remembered, is itself the sum of the other-regarding emotions, can be most profoundly influenced. These mediums are not the formative arts. The chief vehicles of this art have now become the word and the spirit, and its highest expressions, as Sir Martin Conway described, are in literature and similar mediums through which the world is being powerfully moved. Its exponents, therefore, are the master-minds of literature—the seers of the visions of the writers, the poets, the reformers, the teachers who create the mind of the rising generation under the influence of emotion. They are the inspirers of causes, the founders of faiths, the sustainers of the ideal, the authors of those great policies of mind in which the human spirit, rising through contagious emotion from the individual to the universal, is transmitting, through the cultural inheritance, an accumulating power to subordinate itself in civilization to the spiritual meaning which is immanent in the world. And the meaning which underlies it is Power, always Power. It is the systems in which this inspiration lies in its highest might and reality which will win out over all competition in the future of the world.

The characteristic inspiration which is accompanying this development in which the imaginative and emotional literature of the West has become the medium of the highest art, is a very striking phenomenon. In the imaginative literature of all the peoples of the modern West as contrasted with the literature of all other people and all other times, the outstanding feature is the position acceded to woman. In the current literature of the Western world woman stands triumphant as the central figure. In it, as I have stated elsewhere, wherever man becomes an idealist it is almost invariably woman who is the measure of his idealism. It is to the mind of woman that he brings all his ideals, to prove them and to claim support for them. Almost without exception, it is woman who inspires the strongest deeds, the deepest passions, the highest idealisms of men throughout the imaginative literature of our time.

This fact, which is the most distinctive feature of the idealism of the modern West in literature, stands out alike in poetry, in the drama, and in the modern novel. Since the rise of the novel in the sixteenth century, the idealization of Woman is the feature which has grown and deepened in this medium down to the present day. It has made of the novel the predominant form of Western literature. The standard, moreover, which this fact of the idealization of woman has set up in art has become so fundamental that, as I have shown, it has become a canon of art in the modern novel, that man cannot be represented as the higher idealist and woman as the lower cause which has dragged him down, without a sense of artistic disaster and a feeling of failure and outrage being created in the mind of the reader.

The highest expressions of living art in the West are, in short, coming more and more to have a very close relation to the great movements of opinion touched with emotion out of which the world is being organized into larger systems of Power. Genius expressed in its highest form through the medium of art is always the capacity in the artist to render contagious through the emotion of the ideal the power of subduing the immediate world and all its existing interests, to the larger meaning which is conceived to lie in the universal. The highest type of genius in the race has ever been, for this reason, that of the great religious teachers. The tendency in living Western art at present is a tendency through which the function of the artist is again approaching that of the great religious teacher.

The controlling meaning which stands out in this progressive tendency in Western art amounts to this. We are watching in art, under a great number of phases, what I have described as the conscious and infinitely laborious effort of the male mind to reach by slow and painful stages, and by a different road, a position which the mind of woman has already attained in the evolutionary process. In the position which it now occupies, the mind of woman is greatly in advance of the mind of the male of the race, in the development in it of those qualities upon which Power in civilization will rest to an increasing degree in the future.

This clue to the upward transition in art is the clue to progress in all its phases. The advance therein represents the developing challenge to the triumph in the past of the world of the self-regarding emotions. But it is the qualities characteristic of the mind of woman which are bound to form the principal basis of Power in this significant change.

Tolstoy's insight was true when he asserted that it is the ideal of the other-regarding emotions, as seen in that conception of the brotherhood of man which lies behind all the winning developments of civilization, which will supply the dominating influence in Western art in the future. This concept of the oneness of humanity in which the future becomes greater than the present has been, like the concept of God, inherent from the beginning in the process in which evolution is following in history the line of maximum Power. And the upward development which both concepts represent is under all its forms a development towards the ascendancy in the world of qualities that have attained a higher development in the mind of woman than they have reached in the mind of the male.

Progress in the standards of ethics in the West has the same underlying significance as this development which is taking place in the standards of art. Power in civilization, whatever the length and stress of the historical process through which the principle is established, always rests in the last resort on the displacement of the lower standards of ethics by the higher. The character of this development in which the higher standards in ethics are displacing the lower has never been more illuminatingly summarized than in a brief sentence by Green. The command in human conduct, Thou shalt love thy neighbour as thyself, has never varied, said Green in effect; all that *has* varied in the upward progress of humanity is "the practical answer to the question, Who is my neighbour ? "[1]

Progress in ethics is, in short, to be described as the gradual extension of the reach of the other-regarding emotions till it includes the universal. The reasoning capacity of mind has no part in this world-shaping transition. The principal instrument of Power accomplishing the development has consisted always and altogether in qualities of emotion which have their chief expression in the mind of woman. God is the highest concept to which mind is carried by the emotion of the ideal. The command, Thou shalt love the Lord thy God with all thy heart and with all thy soul and with all thy mind, is the highest term of the commandment, Thou shalt love thy neighbour as thyself.

It will be seen at no distant date that the funda-

T. H. Green, *Prolegomena to Ethics*, chap. iii. § 207.

mental mistake made by the leaders of the intellectual movement which has pursued its course in the Western world since the Reformation has consisted in this. In identifying the progress of the world with the development in history of the rationalizing process of mind they have misconceived the basis of Power in civilization. Power in civilization rests ultimately on knowledge which is conveyed through emotion and not through the reasoning processes of mind.

There is a remarkable passage in the literature of the West, in which the blinding light of this conclusion and its bearing is seen as it first flashes on the mind of one of the leading rationalists of our time. In an essay on the influence of the ethic of renunciation as it has been the inspiration of conduct in the great religions, Karl Pearson finds himself towards the conclusion of his argument facing this position. "A predisposition or a prejudice having absolutely no rational basis may," so he puts it, "have a social value and tend to preserve an individual or a group of individuals in the struggle for existence. Do we not here," so he ponders, "catch a glimpse of how a nearly universal predisposition may exist without our being able to give it a rational basis?"[1]   The en-

[1] *Ethic of Free Thought.*

lightened and reasoning individual, he continues, may renounce for himself as untrue or as a delusion the doctrines of sacrifice and subordination as taught by the great religions. "But can such renunciation become a general rule ? *May not the non-renouncing sections ultimately survive ?"*

The answer to Karl Pearson's last question here placed in italics is that by necessity inherent in the evolutionary process, of which Darwin gave us the laws in a lower stage, it is the non-renouncing sections in this sense alone of the race which will ultimately survive. It is an answer which closes the rationalistic controversy in the West. Truth and falsehood in the sense in which Karl Pearson uses them have no meaning. For Truth is the Science of Power. Truth, therefore, does not make its way in the world by controversy or reason. Its standards in the social integration are incomprehensible to the pagan mind. Confronted in the systems of the world with the standards of the pagan era, the exponents of Truth stand like Christ before Pilate's judgment-seat. They answer nothing. They represent the Science of Power. The Facts of the world to which they belong have not yet arrived.

A question which will have risen to the minds of

many throughout this chapter is this : Can it be in
keeping with the order of the evolutionary process
that the mind of woman, which has hitherto occupied
a position of inferiority, should thus become in a
relatively brief period the principal instrument of
Power in the world ?

It may be laid down as a rule in the history of
evolution that all the great developments which
have carried life into new horizons have arisen
in the same way. They were based on qualities
previously developed in obscurity and in conditions
of apparent inferiority. But as soon as the conditions of the new era were assembled in the world,
the qualities which had hitherto appeared inferior
were ready to assume the function which was to
carry the world into an entirely new era of
progress.

Thus it was that the land forms of life, now the
dominant types in the world, were developed from
forms which, though possessing in embryo the
qualities required in the new era, would have appeared to an observer as quite inferior types in the
midst of those then dominant in the ocean. Similarly
among the land types, in the long era of the domin-
ance of the fighting types of life possessing huge
bodies or clothed in defensive armour, there were developed, amongst forms appearing quite subordinate

and inferior at the time, those qualities of brain which were to become the dominant factor in the struggle of types, and which were destined to carry life into new horizons.

So again in the era which dawned in life when the transmission of the accumulated results of past training in the individual became possible through language in the primates, no limited intelligence could have foreseen the nature of the new horizon into which life was to be carried through such qualities developed in conditions of apparent inferiority. For the primates would have appeared to have had stamped upon them all the marks of inferiority and even defeat in the struggle for existence in their adaptation to an arboreal life as a retreat from the forceful ascendant forms which then crowded the plains and valleys of the world. Every comparative student ˙of form and function in the development of life down to the later phases represented in the struggle between races and civilizations, and even in the conflict between human institutions, will be able to multiply these examples indefinitely.

It may be laid down that all the eras of progress in which life has been carried to new horizons have had their origin in qualities developed thus in special conditions, qualities which would have been judged by prevailing standards to be associated with inferiority in the midst of the types then dominant. When the changing conditions of the world offered the opportunity, the qualities thus developed were ready to assume the function suitable to the new era which made the type of life possessing them a dominant one in evolution.

"In the social integration the governing principle slowly rising into sight in the modern struggle of the world is that civilization rests on the social emotion. The principal instrument of the social emotion is the mind of woman. Power in the future of civilization is the science of the organization in society of the emotion of the ideal. The people who first grasp this tremendous lesson in all its practical bearings will have the world at their feet.

This is the lesson which the Emperor William II sought through the elementary school-teachers of Prussia to interpret to civilization in the world-compelling history of modern Germany. The lesson remains in all its mind-subduing significance, despite the calamitous misdirection, despite the tremendous misinterpretation.

I carry to the end of my life the memory of a certain summer afternoon in the year 1908. It was my place to deliver to the University of Oxford the Herbert Spencer Lecture for the year [1] In the restrained and sobered language suitable to the occasion I endeavoured to convey the message I had to deliver. To the audience present I endeavoured gently to break it, that the world into which they had been born was *dead*. Those who were still young, I said, would probably live to see great happenings. The rule of the old individualistic theories of Power upon which the world, and in particular the mind of England, had been nurtured in history had passed for ever. My message was that it was the beliefs and the conceptions possessing the power of organizing the minds of men through long stretches of time into systems of action in which the present was subordinated to an ideal in the future which would rule the world in the times at hand. I did not hesitate to apply the message in the prediction to which I passed. " The next age will probably be the age of the Germanization of the world. For it is those lessons of which the first stages have been displayed in the history of modern Prussia which are likely to be worked out in their fuller applications by successful States in the future." [1]

This message to the mind of England of a few

[1] *Individualism and After*, p. 31.

years ago was as words fallen on sand. Even
William James, who listened to the lecture and
who spoke to me in the name of the United States,
took me to task afterwards for this prophecy.

The world which existed then has been wiped
out of our Western age as if a sponge had closed its
record in history. Its ruling principles have been
deposed. The example of organized Power given
by Germany in the world war which began in 1914
has changed for ever the direction of the main
currents of Western history. It was an example of
stupendous power misconceived and misdirected to
the revival in the West of the ideals of Power characteristic of the pagan past. But the significance
of the example remains for ever in the lesson
which was given to the world as to the almost
superhuman reach of organized Power based on the
emotion of the ideal in the collective mind.

The message which is conveyed to civilization in
this war is in all its fundamental meaning the
message which I attempted to deliver to Oxford in
1908, namely, that Power in the future of the world
will be to the peoples who find the true application
of the lessons of which the first stages have been
displayed in the history of modern Prussia. In this
lesson, the first step is to the knowledge that
Power in the future of civilization is the science

of the emotion of the ideal in the collective mind. The second `step is to the knowledge that the principal instrument in the race of the science of the emotion of the ideal is in the mind of woman.

CHAPTER X

SOCIAL HEREDITY

A S soon as we come to grasp the application of the principle of evolution described in the previous chapters we can hardly fail to perceive that the significance of its bearing on the future of civilization is quite out of the ordinary. The peoples who apply to practical affairs the lessons which are involved will inevitably become the leaders and organizers of the world.

The future science of civilization may be summed up in a sentence. It will be the science of Power. It is waste of time to spend effort discussing other principles of society. There is only one type towards which the universal process of civilization moves—the type of society in which Power is realized to the highest degree. It is therefore of the first importance to grasp firmly the essential facts that distinguish the science of Power in society from the science of Power everywhere else throughout life.

Now it has been already said that Darwinism is

strictly the science only of the evolution of the individual. It is not the science of the evolution of society. This latter science rests fundamentally on a principle which is never encountered in the evolution of the individual. It may be noticed in the world with which Darwin dealt that the mechanism through which Power has been accumulated and perfected in the individual in the rise upwards through orders and types to the highest forms of life is always the same. The entire order of progress rests on the single fact of the continued transmission of the winning qualities from generation to generation through heredity in the individual. In a few words the Darwinian hypothesis may be summarized. We are met in life by the fact of universal variation. Every organism is variable throughout.[1] Darwin exhibited the process of natural selection, sorting out from this variation the characters useful to the individual in the struggle for existence, that is to say, the characters upon which Power rested. The universal means by which the gains of progress thus hall-marked as they arose were held and increased was the transmission of the winning qualities from generation to generation through inborn heredity in the individual. In the

[1] Or as Dr. James Johnstone has recently put it in extreme form, " Every character of an organism or of a part or organ of an organism is variable " (*Science Progress*, April 1916).

Darwinian conception thus all progress rests ultimately upon the mechanism of heredity in the individual.

It is for this reason that Darwinism in all its phases down to the latest Mendelian development is primarily concerned with inborn heredity. It is from the study of the facts and laws governing the transmission of qualities inborn in the individual that modern Darwinians found their claims to have important contributions to make to the science of human society. In the writings and researches of representatives like Galton and Bateson we are accordingly always in the presence of the sustained effort to exhibit the science of society as related to and dependent on the study of the laws of inborn inheritance in the individual. Human progress is presented to us as the scheme of organizing and controlling in the race the mechanism of individual heredity.

When with this feature of current Darwinian teaching in mind we turn now to human society, the first fact which holds attention is perceived to be of great importance as soon as we grasp its application. As society, like the individual, advances in evolution the gains of progress are accumulated and are transmitted from generation to generation by heredity. But here the parallel ceases. The

mechanism of social heredity in no way resembles
the mechanism of inborn heredity.   The mechanism
of inborn heredity is in the individual; the
mechanism of social heredity is outside of the individual.   The medium through which the gains of
progress are held and are transmitted in the individual is inborn at birth, and is in the physical
apparatus of his body as it has come down from the
past.   But the medium through which the gains of
progress are held and transmitted in society is the
accumulated social culture which comes down from
the past.   No part and no quality in this social
inheritance is inborn in the individual.   It is entirely acquired by him from without.   It is imposed
upon him by society in every generation.

Anthropologists have been disputing for a long
time about the fact that the human brain does not
appear for tens of thousands of generations past to
have increased in size or quality in any marked
manner.   What is really meant by one side is that
it has not increased in a manner which corresponds
to the enormous and almost incalculable interval
which separates the results of mind in modern
civilized man from the results of mind in primitive
man ages before the dawn of history.

But the point, the significance of which is nearly
always overlooked in the controversy, is that the

equipment which separates the mind of modern civilized man from the mind of primitive man is almost entirely an equipment which comes to the former through the cumulative social inheritance that he receives from civilization. This inheritance is not inborn in any of us. We have not yet fully grasped the immense import of the fact that *since man became a social creature the winning variations upon which Power has rested in his evolution have been to an ever-increasing degree neither variations in the structure of his body nor in the size of his brain, but variations in the type of social culture to which he is being submitted.*

The importance of the principle here emphasized, namely, that the Power which is characteristic of organized society rests upon and is transmitted through social heredity and does not rest upon and is not transmitted through heredity inborn in the individual, is incalculable. Fifty years hence the attention of civilization will be permanently focused on this distinction as the cardinal fact in the science of Power.

The distinctive conception which in the past has underlain the ideas of modern Darwinians of all schools is that the control and organization of Power in the future of civilization will be in the hands of those who obtain possession of and who direct *o preconceived ends the mechanism of heredity in the individual.   This is a fundamental error.   Those who understand the science of Power in society see that all Power in the future will be in the hands of those who obtain possession of and who direct to preconceived ends not the mechanism of individual heredity but the mechanism of social heredity.   And the instrument of social heredity is the organized Culture of society.

What, therefore, is the peculiar nature of social heredity, and what have we to do to obtain possession of this source of omnipotent power in the future of civilization ?

The marked features of social heredity in which it differs absolutely from that inborn heredity upon which Darwinians and many general theorists have attempted in the past to found a science of society are as follows.   In inborn heredity the constituent qualities tend to be indefinitely persistent and difficult to alter.   Despite all the work which has been done on the subject we have not yet arrived at any real knowledge or control of the causes of variation.   The deeper our acquaintance with the subject the more clearly we perceive its uncertainties and its limited possibilities.[1]   Slow

[1] The recent utterances of Bateson on the subject, and there is no one whose knowledge of the facts and principles under-

change can only be produced in the elements of inborn heredity in the manner in which breeders attempt to produce change in plants and animals and in conditions which we can foresee to be quite impossible in human society in the future.

With the elements of social heredity everything is different. We can perceive at once, as soon as we grasp the principles of the subject, that it is along this line, namely, through the control of social heredity, that mind will ultimately direct the course of human evolution. For social heredity resting on mind is the direct basis of Power where Power will be supreme, namely, in its collective expressions. The most revolutionary change can be effected in a brief space of time through control of the elements of social heredity. The cause and agency of variation are here absolutely under the direction of mind. We can foresee that the control of social heredity will be practicable. And through the control of the elements of social heredity it will be an ideal not impossible of realization to transform the world in the lifetime of a few generations.

It is now some fifty years since one of the most

lying it goes further, are full of caution. "That species have come into existence by an evolutionary process no one seriously doubts; but few who are familiar with the facts that genetic research has revealed are now inclined to speculate as to the manner by which the process has been accomplished" (*The Problem of Genetics*, by William Bateson, F.R.S.).

blighting and retrograde conceptions which ever influenced the mind of civilization came to obtain wide currency in the West. As soon as the Darwinian hypothesis was accepted it was correctly perceived that it made all change and progress in life dependent on the laws of inheritance in the individual. At the same time it exhibited the qualities thus transmitted by inborn heredity as relatively so fixed and unchangeable that they were to be considered as almost beyond control in the lifetime of the individual.

Up to the time that Darwin published the *Origin of Species* a different idea had been widely prevalent in Western thought and particularly in all teachings founded on the characteristic religious beliefs of the West—that the mind of each generation as represented in the child was practically a blank sheet upon which good or evil might be written in the future according to the nature of the training or the nature of the education to which the young were subjected. Human character was presented in this conception as the result of training, and the note which underlay the effort of nearly all social and religious reformers had been a note of emphasis on the paramount importance of the environment in which the young were to be reared and educated.

One of the most revolutionary results of the

Darwinian hypothesis in the West was to undermine and discredit this conception. There was, of course, no doubt as to the transmission of inborn qualities by heredity in human beings just as in animals and in plants. But this fact came to obscure almost entirely to Darwinians the immensely more important fact that the qualities upon which efficiency and Power rest in collective evolution as distinct from individual evolution are qualities of *character* which are almost exclusively imposed and transmitted through social heredity. For a period of years the fact was completely lost sight of in science that the upward progress of the world in civilization rested on qualities in the individual imposed on the individual from without, and not on the nature of ancestral heredity inborn within him.

The influence of the retrograde Darwinian conception spread with lightning-like rapidity throughout Western thought. Darwinians like Galton, through a series of writings which attained wide publicity, fixed general attention in a marked manner on the nature of inborn heredity and brought forward ambitious schemes for the improvement of the race, conceived, not as in the past as dependent on the training and education of the young, but on success in selecting and breeding from the required strains of heredity in individuals after the manner of breeders of stock animals. Social reformers who accepted Galton's standpoint began, like Karl Pearson in the passages before quoted, to enlarge on the peculiar nature of inborn heredity in the individual and on the great length of time required to produce any fundamental change in human nature.

Within a short time the imaginative literature of the West was deeply affected. It became tinged throughout with the idea of biological predestination. The idea of the persistence and the relative unchangeableness of qualities in human nature resting on inborn heredity became a dominant note, uttered now, as it seemed, with authority coming direct from the leaders of science   The quality of inevitableness in inborn heredity conceived as overruling all the elements of motive and intention imposed on the individual by training was soon perceived to be a principle in art which was capable of yielding profound dramatic effect.

In the literature of Great Britain, Russia, Germany, and other countries it began to be used with telling effect in the novel and the drama. The dominating influence of inborn heredity was one of the principal conceptions through which a writer of international influence like Ibsen deeply moved the mind of the West. The Norwegian dramatist used it with powerful effect in some situations, as where in the play *Ghosts* he makes the tendencies of evil inborn heredity coming down through the father overbear in the son in the presence of the mother all the effects of training and religion imposed through life on the son.

In the writings of another author of international fame, like Anatole France, the conception of the determining influence of inborn heredity and its power to override in the individual all the effects of prolonged training became an instrument in the hands of genius through which the faith of a whole people was made to feel humiliated and abashed. There is no more poignant and cynical drama of human defeat than that exhibited by Anatole France in the story of the material and spiritual ruin of the Bishop of Trinqueballe who, after recalling from death three children of tender age but of evil parentage, caused them to be trained and educated in his own saintly principles. The inevitableness with which the gifted French writer made the elements of inborn heredity in the children to develop and in the end to completely triumph over the influences imposed on them by the Bishop through training and education is one of the most striking examples of the working of a principle in art which is capable of producing intense dramatic effects but which gradually shocked, startled, and in the end deeply impressed for evil the average mind throughout the West.

As the movement ran its course in literature its effects became many sided. Following in the wake of the Darwinian development, conclusions about the effects of inborn heredity, such as were reached in the study of diseases by medical researchers, in the study of crime by criminologists like Lombroso, in the study of inheritance in plants and animals by Mendelians like Bateson, tended to be carried in literature far beyond their legitimate applications. They were made by imaginative theorists to supply the basis for vague, far-reaching generalizations about human society, and about races and nations, and even about civilization as a whole, the effect of which on the general mind throughout the West was profoundly disintegrating and demoralizing.

The movement came in time to influence widely social and political affairs even in world-wide aspects. Darwin's cousin, Francis Galton, the founder of the branch of study to which he gave the name of Eugenics, may be said more than any single individual to have helped to give direction to theories about the effect of inborn heredity in peoples and races which it has taken the results of the two greatest wars in the world's history to counteract and permanently discredit in the Western mind.

Five years before Darwin published the *Origin of Species*, Galton in his *Narrative of an Explorer in Tropical South Africa* was giving wide currency to the view that the vast difference between the position in the world of the advanced and less advanced races was due to a corresponding difference in their inborn mental qualities. The inborn mental faculties of aboriginal peoples, like the intelligent Damara tribes amongst whom he travelled in South Africa, was made by him the starting-point for generalizations which were widely repeated throughout civilization.

Galton formed a very low estimate of the mental capacity of peoples like the Damaras. The evidence upon which his conclusions were formed was mainly evidence to the fact that they could not count. When bartering for cattle, the Damaras appeared to have no conception of number. Two sticks of tobacco had to be put into the native's hand and one sheep driven away, and then another two sticks and the second sheep driven away, or he could not follow the transaction. Galton described how he observed a Damara floundering hopelessly in a calculation of this sort, while his own spaniel which had new-born puppies from which two or three had been removed was equally confused. She evidently, said Galton, had a vague notion of counting, but in the two attempts to grasp the nature of numbers, Galton remarked, " the comparison reflected no great honour on the man." [1]

That the members even of the highest civilized race when without the artificial enumeration scale inherited from civilization have no more natural ability to count than the Damara whom Galton observed ; that the children of African aborigines, and even the children of the aborigines of Australia, learn when taught the same things quite as easily and readily as the children of Europeans ; and that the apparent difference which he noted between the mental faculties of the advanced and less-advanced races of the world was due to the nature of their social inheritance and not to the nature of their inborn faculties, were matters which were beyond the horizon of Galton's mind at the time.

The standpoint in these matters of men of Galton's calibre was accepted widely throughout the educated world of the West. It was a firm belief at the time among a certain type of Galton's fellow-countrymen that the Englishman had a vast inborn mental superiority over other peoples with which he came in contact. Other nations held like beliefs about themselves. Informed and cultured Russians

[1] *Narrative of an Explorer in Tropical South Africa.*

before the Russo-Japanese War spoke habitually of a people like the Japanese as yellow monkeys. A similar habit of mind pervaded in great strength the characteristic type of German literature which led up to the world war that opened in 1914. In all its phases that literature in Germany may be observed to have been saturated with the influence of the assumption that the Germanic races possessed some inborn mental heredity which made them superior to other peoples.

When the question is asked, What basis is there for the conception, thus put forward under so many recent forms in the West, which sets up inborn heredity as the determining influence in the evolution of civilization? The answer must be emphatic. The idea has no permanent basis in knowledge. The movement in the West which has essayed to establish the science of human progress on the control and organization of any peculiar inborn heredity either in races or in individuals is based on illusion. It is a movement which has given rise to one of the most pernicious and reactionary developments which has characterized the Western world for five centuries.

In the evolution of Power in civilization the heredity which controls everything is the *social* heredity which is transmitted through *social* culture.

The greatest lesson which modern Germany has taught civilization in the world war which began in 1914 is not any of the lessons upon which attention has been mainly concentrated. It is the lesson that the collective heredity which is transmitted through culture is the master principle of the world. Every inborn quality in a people is ultimately subordinate to this social heredity. For the highest of all abilities with which a people can be equipped is the ability to organize and to subordinate themselves to the kind of culture upon which Power rests and which is always transmitted through the social heredity. There has been no people in the world who has possessed in a higher degree the power of subordinating themselves to the social heredity transmitted through culture than the German peoples. If it had been the fortune of those peoples to have had impressed upon them, preceding the outbreak of the war of 1914, an enlightened culture there is no goal in civilization to which they might not successfully have aspired.

The social heredity transmitted through social culture is infinitely more important to a people than any heredity inborn in the individuals thereof. It is through collective heredity that the long sequences of cause and effect upon which Power rests are imposed on the human mind in civilization.

18

Through the organization of an ideal transmitted through this social heredity any result whatever that may be aimed at may be produced in the world. The science of heredity transmitted through culture is the science of Power upon which the attention of all who desire to change the world will be concentrated in the future. Let us turn therefore and look at some of the facts which help us to understand the first principles of this science.

For the past fifteen years I have been engaged on a series of experiments on heredity which exhibit the reach and influence of social heredity as distinct from inborn heredity in a manner which it is of the first importance to understand. The attention of science has been so exclusively directed in the past to the study of inborn heredity that as a rule no other kind of heredity has been discussed or even thought of. This has been particularly so in the case of animals. One of the most interesting results obtained in these experiments was that the heredity of every species of wild animal upon which I experimented was found to consist of two kinds, inborn heredity and social heredity. The latter was nearly always found to be the most striking and the most important in its effects.

There has been no more widely held idea in the past than that the characteristic habits of any species of wild animals which persist under all conditions are the results of heredity which is inborn in all the individuals of the species. For instance, one of the most persistent and dominant of the characteristics peculiar to wild animals is that quality, held to be inborn, which is called instinctive fear of natural enemies. Darwinians have dealt at great length with this instinct. At first sight it appears to be an obvious example of inborn heredity, developed by natural selection. For individuals which did not possess it would always tend, it was said, to be weeded out and to leave no descendants. Fear of natural enemies is one of the most powerful of the instincts existing in wild animals, and it usually appears to be so deeply registered in the physical basis of the animal's mind that it is nearly always ineradicable by training in the adult.

Now anyone who is acquainted with the literature of this subject, and who recalls how Darwinians like Romanes dwell on fear of natural enemies in animals as an inborn inheritance transmitted from ancestors in whom it was developed by natural selection, will probably experience great surprise if he turns to one of the most valuable and interesting records of observation and experiment on animals published in recent years, namely, the *Childhood of Animals,* by Dr. P. Chalmers Mitchell, F R.S., Secretary to the Zoological Society, London.

The natural enemy, which of all others probably preys on the largest number of species of animals throughout the world, and which should, therefore, be the most universally recognized through inborn heredity, is the snake in all its varieties. The idea that animals of nearly all kinds recognize the snake with panic and terror by inborn instinct has been one of the most widely accepted ideas in the past. It is of exceptional interest therefore to find that a large series of Dr. Chalmers Mitchell's experiments in the Zoological Gardens is directed to testing the existence in animals of an inborn instinct of fear for this almost universal enemy of birds and mammals in the greater part of the world.

The first fact established by Dr. Chalmers Mitchell's experiments is remarkable. His observations were concerned at the outset with the considerable number of species of animals which are usually given in the Zoological Gardens to the snakes as food, the victims being placed alive in the cages. The noteworthy fact is recorded that in the case of every one of the species of animals experimented with, there was observed, to use Dr. Chalmers Mitchell's words, " no special dread of snakes nor the slightest instinctive fear or foreknowledge of their approaching doom."

The experiments were then conducted on a wider scale, and Dr. Chalmers Mitchell continued : " Moreover, nearly every kind of mammal that we tried was indifferent to snakes. Guinea-pigs and rats would run over them ; a hyrax, which is both intelligent and which from living in trees and on rocks must often encounter snakes, was hardly even interested. . . . Small carnivores, dogs, foxes, and wolves, sheep, antelopes, and deer, zebras and donkeys, were either quite indifferent or came up to the bars and sniffed," and, on finding the snake was not something to eat, " moved away with an air of wearied disgust." Frogs, which form the natural food of snakes in this country, showed not the slightest trace of instinctive fear. The lower monkeys also showed no general instinctive knowledge or fear of snakes.

This is a most striking record from an observer of the experience and standing of Dr. Chalmers Mitchell. The large number and the representative character of the species experimented with will be noticed. The experiments as a whole give results which are directly in the face of previous general assumptions—that is to say, in the representative species of animals above mentioned there was found no trace of any transmission from ancestors of inborn fear or recognition of such a universal natural enemy as the snake. Even the few cases mentioned by Dr. Chalmers Mitchell as forming the exception to the rule indicated have probably an explanation which goes to confirm the general result of the experiments as a whole.[1]

Whence, therefore, comes this most powerfully developed instinct of fear of natural enemies which is undoubtedly almost universally present at an early age under certain conditions in all the individuals of wild species ? I will proceed to the answer.

I turn now to my own experiments, which were conducted over a long period of time and in which care was taken to exclude disturbing influences. They are in many respects even more remarkable than those just referred to. I experimented with a

---

[1] The exceptions mentioned by Dr. Chalmers Mitchell were some of the higher monkeys and a few of the more intelligent passerine birds. These appeared to Dr. Chalmers Mitchell to show the same instinctive recognition of snakes that most human beings are said to display. As the result of my own observations in South Africa, I have the strongest doubt as to whether there is in the human child any fear of snakes which represents inborn heredity recognizing an ancestral enemy. What is however present from an earlier age in the child is simply the intelligent brain which distinguishes in the unusual appearance and movements of the snake a suggestion of exceptional power and danger. I feel sure that it is the same explanation and not inborn heredity recognizing an ancestral enemy which applies to the behaviour of the more intelligent passerine birds and the higher monkeys as mentioned by Dr. Chalmers Mitchell.

number of wild species of British birds and mammals. In none of them did I find any trace in the young of an inborn, instinctive fear of the natural enemies which were regarded with fear and terror by the adult of the species. Young wild hares and young wild rabbits showed no inborn fear of either dogs or cats. Young wild rabbits and young wild hares became as friendly and playful from the beginning with specially trained cats to which they were introduced as if they had been all of the same species. Young rabbits, showing no inborn fear of dogs, would frisk and play with the hereditary enemy of their kind by whom their species had been hunted for tens of thousands of generations. The young of our common wild birds showed no inborn fear of the cat when, fully fledged, they were under proper conditions introduced to it for the first time. Nor did they develop any fear afterwards. And so also when they were introduced under similar conditions to birds of prey like the hawk or the carrion crow trained to friendly relations.

If it be asked now whence comes the universal and ineradicable fear of natural enemies, which is present under natural conditions in the whole of the adult members of the species in these cases, the answer is of great interest. The conclusion which I arrived at was that in the numerous typical wild species experimented upon the whole of this powerful influence, representing a most dominant and ineradicable habit of animal nature, was entirely the result of social heredity imposed on the young of each generation by training and example and nearly always under conditions of strong emotion.

As the experiments were extended it was found, also in the face of generally accepted ideas, that in many cases deep-seated habits of species, extending even to such fundamental matters as the nature of their food and the usual manner of living, were not matters of inborn heredity but were acquired as part of the social inheritance which the adults of the species imposed by example and training on the young of each generation. Once acquired the habits were as fixed and unchangeable as those which are the result of inborn heredity. But it was found that a different habit, proving equally unchangeable once acquired, could be imposed in the beginning in the same way.

It has been already pointed out that the distinctive characteristic of social heredity, as contrasted with inborn heredity, is that the elements of social heredity can be completely changed and different elements imposed in a short time. It became evident in these experiments that, if control could be obtained of the social heredity of a species, many of its apparently ingrained and fixed habits could be entirely changed in a single generation.

The case of a wild species of New Zealand parrot which, although previously vegetarian, acquired after the introduction of European sheep the habit of feeding on the kidney fat of these animals, causing the death of the sheep which it attacked, is often quoted as an extraordinary example in nature of a sudden change in the fundamental habit of life in a wild species.   But there can be no doubt that sudden changes equally deep seated in the habits of a whole species could be effected at will by obtaining control of its social heredity.

Many of the experiments gave the strongest indications in this direction. There is no more established vegetarian British bird than our common wood pigeon.   In one of my experiments with the young of this species a young bird was brought up with a carrion crow and a hawk which were fed on raw meat.   The young pigeon by example was led to feed on the same food, and throve on the exclusively meat diet.   So fixed did the habit thus acquired by social heredity become that when the adult pigeon at a later stage was offered the grains which formed the natural diet of its species it did not recognize them as food.

The common wild hare never makes a burrow in its natural state. But when a young wild hare was brought up with rabbits, which did not show it the hostility which is usual between the species, the young hare acquired from its companions the habit of burrowing and would cast the earth excavated with forepaws backwards between its hind legs exactly in the manner of a rabbit.

When there was any physiological insufficiency in the organs of an animal to prevent it from acquiring or maintaining the habit usually imposed by social heredity results of this kind did not follow. It was found for instance that a diet of grains could not be imposed by any effect of example on meat-eating birds. But the striking fact which has to be emphasized is that, where no natural physiological insufficiency existed, the most unexpected habits could easily be imposed on young animals by example and training. And further, the habits so imposed were found to be transmitted again to the next generation through ordinary social heredity.

Some grasp of the manner in which the elements of social heredity are imposed on the young under conditions of the strongest emotion, and some perception of the extraordinary reach and strength of the habits thus imposed, may be obtained from the study of an example which exhibits the facts clearly in relation to their bearing upon the subject of social heredity in human society.

One of the species of wild animals with which a considerable series of my experiments was concerned was the wild duck. There is probably no creature which has been more universally hunted by man from primeval times than the wild duck. The adult bird is one of the shyest of creatures. In alertness and craftiness in her nesting habits, in 'he tricks and stratagems for avoiding pursuit which both the parent and the young have developed, this ancestor of our breed of domestic ducks has few equals in the wild. It breeds plentifully in remote places, usually near water, throughout northern Europe, and in all my experiments eggs or newly hatched young were taken from the nests of the wild birds in their native haunts. In all the experiments I found no evidence that some of the most characteristic habits of the wild duck were the result of inborn heredity developed by natural selection. On the contrary, the experiments furnished evidence from which it was impossible to avoid the conclusion that the habits were transmitted by social inheritance imposed on the young mainly under conditions of strong emotion.

The record of a single example will exhibit the meaning that was found to be inherent in a great number of experiments. I came on a nest of the wild duck in a marsh as the young birds had just emerged from the eggs. The mother duck flew off and disappeared in the sedge, flapping a wing to which she pretended injury. I stood by the nest for some hours and watched the young birds. The greater number were already active and displaying an interest in their surroundings. They began to try to get out of the nest, and I took them one by one in my hand and placed them in the water, where in the stillness that reigned they splashed and twittered and enjoyed themselves. They showed not the slightest fear of me, nestling from time to time on my feet, and turning intelligent eyes upwards to look at me, evidently quite ready to accept me in the fullest confidence as their guardian.

The wild duck had been in these marshes for untold ages. She had been here even in the days when the woolly rhinoceros left its remains with those of the cavemen in the adjacent hills. During all this time her kind had been one of the most universally hunted among wild creatures. The spent cartridges of the modern sportsmen strewed the bog around. Yet here were her offspring just entering on the world and showing no sign of any kind of any inborn fear of this the hereditary enemy of the species. After a time I moved away some distance to

watch what would happen. The mother bird
returned and alighted near by. The little ducks
rushed towards her as she called. I could observe
her. She was chattering with emotion. Every
feather was quivering with excitement. The Great
Terror of Man was upon her. After a short interval
I advanced towards the group again. The mother
bird flew away with a series of loud warning quacks.
The little ones scattered to cover, flapping their short
wing stumps, and with beaks wide open cheeping in
terror. 'With difficulty I found one of them again
in hiding. It was now a wild, transformed
creature trembling in panic which could not be
subdued.

It is in this way, and under conditions of the
strongest emotion, that the accumulated experience of tens of thousands of generations of the
species is imposed on young birds. Once having
received it, within a few days, even within a few
hours, they pass into another world from which they
can never be reclaimed. In the numerous experiments with wild ducks which I made, the following
conclusions stood out without any exception. The
little ducks, hatched out from the eggs taken from
the nest, or taken themselves from the nest the first
day after hatching, knew nothing of any fear of man,
and they never acquired it afterwards if brought up

with domestic birds.[1]   But when once the Terror had been transmitted to them through the social heredity of their species they could not afterwards be tamed.   When brought up by a foster-parent the young wild ducks acquired that exact relationship of friendliness to man which the foster-parent displayed and which differed considerably according to the birds used as foster-parents.

I have found from observations in many countries and on different animals that it is in the same way that the exact distance up to which wild animals will allow man to approach them is always imposed on the young through social heredity.   It represents the accumulated experience of the species in the past. The manner in which the inheritance is imposed on the young in every generation may be watched even in the streets of London in the case of the common sparrow.   When the young sparrows leave the nest they are comparatively tame.   But they are watched on the ground assiduously by the parents, and when an enemy like man approaches to within a certain distance, the cock parent utters a loud shrill note expressing strong emotion which causes the

[1] Darwin, noting that "young chickens have lost that fear of the dog and cat which no doubt was originally instinctive in them," and perceiving the difficulty of explaining such a change solely as due to selection, attributes it to an "inherited change in mental habit" (*Origin of Species*, chap. viii.).

young birds instantly to take flight. The exact
distance to which man is allowed to approach is the
danger limit fixed by the long accumulated experience of the species, which is thus transmitted to the
young and which is fixed in them ineradicably
under conditions of emotion. But when a group of
tamed birds is isolated and the social heredity is
thus changed, it is found that the altered inheritance is similarly transmitted to future generations.

The supreme interest of the foregoing facts is
not in their relation to any of the problems of
animal life. Their great importance lies in the
application which they bear to the highest and most
vital problems of human society. When we remember how few and unimportant are the examples
of the social state among the higher animals below
man, the unexpected magnitude of the part played
by social heredity even in such conditions has great
significance. If social heredity thus transmitted
anew to the young in every generation is the agency
through which there may be imposed and fixed on
whole species possessing no distinctive social habits
some of the most characteristic qualities of these
species, and if these qualities ineradicable in the individual can nevertheless be entirely replaced in another
generation by quite different qualities, similarly imposed by social heredity, what then must be the un-

imagined importance of social heredity in a creature like man whose almost unlimited power on the horizon before him in civilization rests exclusively on the potentiality of mind in the social state ?

As the observations on social heredity begun with animals were carried into human society, the first fact encountered was very remarkable. Notwithstanding the supreme importance of social heredity in the evolution of civilization, there has not been in the past any wide or systematic study of it conducted on modern scientific lines. Nearly all the research work on the subject of heredity in human society that has been done in the past consists of experiments, observations, and discussions concerned almost exclusively with the relatively less important subject of inborn heredity. In much of this work also, as in a considerable proportion of Galton's observations and in the studies of many writers in criminology, the subject of inborn heredity and of social heredity is almost inextricably confused.

My own studies of social heredity were undertaken with the definite object of endeavouring to distinguish, as in animals, between the effects of inborn heredity and the effects of social heredity. They were conducted in various parts of the world amongst aboriginal races, ruling races, aristocracies, subject peoples, and slave peoples. They were extended to various grades and classes of society in the United Kingdom, to boys embraced in the boy scout movement, and to children at schools and public institutions. In all the studies I was concerned primarily with the subject of collective heredity in its relation to Power in civilization.

I will not discuss at length here the first conclusion to which researches of this kind are bound to carry the observer at an early stage. I have referred to it with some emphasis elsewhere.[1] In the face of the evidence which is to hand on all sides it is impossible to avoid being convinced that none of the leading races or nationalities which have ruled in the past or which wield power on a large scale over other peoples in the present have done so, or do so now, because of any distinctive superior intellectual faculties inborn in the ruling race. The ideas on this subject which prevailed a few generations ago will not survive the test of being brought into contact with facts.

Turning first to aboriginal races, Galton's hasty generalizations about what he conceived to be the greatly inferior mentality of aboriginal races like the Damaras have become, when submitted to

[1] *Social Evolution*, ch. ix.

examination in the light of facts, no more than nonsense. In nearly all the British colonies, where aboriginal children of various races are educated in elementary schools under the same conditions as European children, it is in evidence in the published State records that the former learn just as easily and readily as European children, and are capable of showing equally good examination results. The same is true of the negro children in the public elementary schools of the United States.

Coming to higher education and to the results displayed in conditions where students of European races are trained and educated for the higher activities of the world side by side with representatives of almost all the leading peoples outside Europe, the facts are equally noteworthy.

At many centres of university and higher education in England, and at a large number of centres of learning and higher training on the continent of Europe, students of Indian, Japanese, Burmese, Siamese, Chinese, Negro, and many other races are to be found undergoing preparation for the higher professions and for the superior work of the world under exactly the same conditions as students of European races. The results go to show that non-European students quite hold their own in intellectual achievement in comparison with European students. When every allowance is made for the fact that the non-European students are often selected representatives of large numbers, there remains nevertheless no evidence to which weight can be given tending to establish the existence of any inborn quality of superior intellect in the students of European races. More than once in my inquiries experienced and competent observers, familiar with the capacities of students of various races in University or Bar examinations in England, have expressed to me the opinion that it would be impossible to make out a serious case for accepting the existence of any inborn intellectual superiority in the English students, and that if such an opinion were urged the case would be quite as strong for holding the opposite view.

Confining attention to the peoples who have played a ruling part in the history of the Western world in the past, it would in the same manner be impossible to make out a case for inborn intellectual pre-eminence in any one of them over other European races. In the face of world-wide evidence it would be entirely foolish to attempt to maintain that the Teutonic peoples possessed inborn intellectual superiority over the Celts, or the Celts over the Slavs, or the Slavs in turn over the Teutons. It would be equally absurd in face of the evidence to maintain that any European people possessed inborn intellectual superiority over the Jews.

Facts of the same significance are encountered if the scrutiny is restricted to the different races which combine to make up any of the political aggregates that have played a great part in the development of Europe. The Saxon and Norman peoples have probably, on the whole, performed a larger practical part in the development of Great Britain and of the British Empire than the Celtic peoples with whom they have been so closely associated in history. But so far as there are any grounds for estimating separately the achievement of the different races in Great Britain, it would represent a claim in face of the facts of history to assert that there is proof of any superior intellectual faculty inborn in peoples of Saxon or Norman descent in comparison with peoples of Celtic descent.

Conditions of the same kind are encountered amongst the races who make up the peoples of Germany. In modern Germany it is often pointed out by Germans themselves that notwithstanding the ruling part played by Prussia in the evolution of the modern German Empire the intellectual part of the work has not rested to any corresponding degree with natives of Prussia. The two men who more than any others created the intellectual ethos in which the deeds of modern Prussia became possible were Treitschke and Nietzsche, neither of whom was Prussian in descent. A very large proportion of the thinkers and leaders of Prussia have not been Prussians. It is curious to note, remarks a recent writer,[1] "that the majority of Prussian figures that have held the Western imagination have not been Prussian by birth, and have seldom been even Germanic in origin."

In none of the dominant peoples of the world to-day, and in none of the ruling races which have been prominent in history in the past, is the basis of Power to be found in inborn intellectual superiority over the peoples ruled. What, therefore, is the basis of Power in human history ?

The answer to this question carries us very far. In arriving at it, the belief, which prevailed in the popular mind throughout the West until recently, as to the inborn nature of the causes establishing superiority in races, and the prepossessions as to the controlling importance of inborn heredity in ruling races and ruling peoples, of the kind which have come down to us in England through Galton in science and through Freeman in the teaching of history, will have to be abandoned. There can be no doubt that the

[1] F. M. Hueffer, *When Blood is their Argument*, Part I. chap. II. § ii.

first essential in the constitution of Power in all the forms through which Power expresses itself in the history of races and of peoples lies in the elements of their social heredity. The character of a people is formed by the nature of its social heredity. *It is the nature of its social heredity which creates a ruling people. It is what it lacks in its social heredity that relegates a people to the position of an inferior race.*

In the national and racial inheritance of a people the influence of the elements of its social heredity insensibly envelops and saturates the entire collective mind. Imposed on the young at an early age and under conditions of emotion the effects of inheritance thus transmitted exceed and outlast those of every other influence in life. It was with well-founded instinct that William II of Germany on his accession turned to the elementary school teachers of his country when he aimed to impose the elements of a new social heredity on the whole German people. The result was the concentration of mind and the extraordinary collective strength with which Germany went into the world war in 1914.

The higher end was missed by William II.[1] But

[1] Mazzini penetrated further towards the central principles of Power in the coming era of civilization, when from 1840 onwards

it remains in full view of the world. Civilization
is absolutely invincible once it realizes the secret
of its own unity. The main cause of those deep
dividing differences which separate peoples and
nationalities and classes from each other and which
prevent or stultify collective effort in all its most
powerful forms lies exclusively in the nature of
the social heredity which is imposed on the young.
In a generation they could all be swept away if
civilization put before itself the will to impose on
the young the ideal of subordination to the common
aims of organized humanity.

The influence of a collective ideal imposed on the
mind of the young under conditions of emotion is
incalculable. It is the only cause capable of bringing into action the deepest strength of which human
nature is capable. Every individual in the mass
is continuously driven by it to endeavour to lift
himself to the level of his inner ideal social self
exactly in the manner described by William James
in his *Text Book of Psychology*,[1] but driven now
towards a collective instead of towards an individual
he was outlining to the Italian working classes the maxims under
which their progress towards emancipation in history must proceed. " Your task is to form the universal family. . . . Humanity
is the living word of God. . . . Religions govern the world . . .
Seek in Woman strength, inspiration, a redoubling of your moral
faculties. . . . Education, this is the great word which sums up
our whole doctrine" (*On the Duties of Man*, VIII , III., II., I.).

[1] *Text Book of Psychology*, chap. xii.

end. The influence affects all the processes of mind. It colours and directs in after life the conclusions of the thinker so that these are in reality predetermined in him by the emotion of an ideal imposed on him at an earlier stage. The influence reaches to the uttermost workings of mind, so that in the development of abstract systems of thought the main problem which has continually beset the mind of the philosopher in history is simply, as Leslie Stephen has described it, " how conclusions which are agreeable to his emotions can be connected with postulates which are congenial to his intellect."

In nations the inheritance transmitted in social heredity may be very complex. Geographical, economic, and material causes of many kinds may contribute important factors to it. But the essential element of Power in all social heredity is the emotion of the ideal. Once effectively imposed, this idealism becomes the expression of the living soul of a people. Its influence cannot be estimated. It subordinates everything. It becomes Power incarnate. There is no object which a people or a race can set before itself which is not possible of attainment through the organization and the transmission of an ideal in its social heredity. In the days when modern Germany was on the anvil

the chief conception underlying all the lectures of
the teacher who above all others expressed the soul
of Germany was that which drew the rising generation of young German students to Treitschke. It
was expressed in the saying that the most precious
natural possession that a people can hold is its
idealism,[1] and in the sustained assertion, that any
aim that a living people aspires to, that aim it
will infallibly attain.[2]

It was in this way that Japan achieved the
greatest miracle in modern civilization by re-creating
herself, and in a few decades transforming herself
into a surprising vehicle of Power. It was in this
manner that modern Germany astonished humanity
by transforming herself within two generations
into a potentiality for good or evil which eclipsed
that of ancient Rome. Only through the character
of her idealism did Germany fail to reach the world
goal at which she aimed. The leaders who imposed
the mechanism of Power on her missed the chief
knowledge of the law of Power in civilization, namely,
that the winning type of Power rests on the principles which subordinate us to the universal. If
her leaders had grasped this central fact of human
evolution there is no dream that the German peoples

[1] *Essay on Freedom*, by Heinrich von Treitschke.
[2] *The Life of Treitschke*, by Adolf Hausrath.

had dreamed that Germany would not have realized in the modern world.

The will to attain to an end imposed on a people by the emotion of an ideal organized and transmitted through social heredity is the highest capacity of mind. It can only be imposed in all its strength through the young. So to impose it has become the chief end of education in the future.

Oh, you blind leaders who seek to convert the world by laboured disputations! Step out of the way or the world must fling you aside. Give us the Young. Give us the Young and we will create a new mind and a new earth in a single generation.

The idealism which will win out in the stress of the world is that through which Power must obtain the completest expression. Power in its highest expression is the science of organizing the individual mind in the service of the universal. Truth is nothing else than this science of Power. This is the test by which every religion will have to stand or fall.

A CHART OF HUMAN PROGRESS

A CHART OF HUMAN PROGRESS

THE SURVIVAL OF THE FITTEST

THE FEATURES.	IN THE LOWER OR INDIVIDUAL STAGE OF HUMAN EVOLUTION. (Laws as described by Darwin.)	IN THE HIGHER OR SOCIAL STAGE OF HUMAN EVOLUTION. (Laws as described by Kidd.)
The fittest are . . .	Those possessing the power to *Secure most efficiently* the interests of Self in the Struggle for Survival.	Those possessing the power to *Sacrifice most efficiently* the interests of Self in the Struggle for Survival.
The result of the Survival of the Fittest is	The gradual perfecting in the individual of every quality contributing to *His own efficiency* in pursuit of self-interest.	The gradual perfecting in the individual of every quality contributing to *Collective efficiency* in all human institutions.
The Centre of Gravity in all Human Institutions is	*In the Present.* It is the era of the ascendancy of those limited interests which rest ultimately on *Force,* and which are all driven by the law of their being toward *Absolutism.*	*In the Future.* It is the era of the ascendancy of all those universal interests which rest ultimately on *Tolerance,* and which are all driven by the law of their being toward *Freedom.*

The Motive quality in Human Evolution is	*Reason.* Science in this stage being the reasoned knowledge of Force.	*The Emotion of the Ideal.* Art, of which the highest phase is religion, being in this stage the emotional knowledge of the Universal.
The Dominant Factor in Human Evolution is	*The Capacity of the fighting Male.*	*The Mind of Woman.*
The Principle of Efficiency in Human Institutions is	*The Spirit of aggressive War.* The increasing incompatibility of this spirit with the efficiency of collective institutions gradually becomes manifest.	*The Spirit of the Child-Mind.* The increasing ascendancy of this spirit as the basis of efficiency in all collective institutions gradually becomes marked.
Other characteristic Features are	(1) The world is capable only of very slow change. (2) It is based on the limited potentialities of heredity transmitted from individual to individual through the medium of the body (individual inheritance). (3) A condition in which the ruling motion of men is the desire to acquire property in fight. (4) A condition of increasing poverty at one pole and accumulating property at the other.	(1) The world can be absolutely transformed in a single generation. (2) It is based on the unlimited potentialities of heredity transmitted from generation to generation through the medium of mind (social inheritance). (3) A condition in which the emotion of the Ideal, organised through public opinion and directed through the young in education, is omnipotent. (4) A condition in which the programmes of all progressive governments move towards the exploitation of the resources of the world on the basis of Brotherhood, and responsibility to each other as it prevails in the Family.

INDEX

PRINTED BY
MORRISON AND GIBB LIMITED
EDINBURGH

CPSIA information can be obtained
at www.ICGtesting.com
Printed in the USA
BVHW041217130121
597730BV00004B/138